teen
mental
health
.org

March 2015

This is the updated version of the Mental Health and High School Curriculum Guide (the Guide) and supports the web based lesson plans and teaching resources found at:

http://teenmentalhealth.org/curriculum/

The password is: **t33nh3alth**

This version of the Guide has been created by Dr. Stan Kutcher and Ms. Yifeng Wei of Dalhousie University and the IWK Health Center. Dr. Stan Kutcher, MD; FRCPC, FCAHS, is Professor of Psychiatry, the Sun Life Financial Chair in Adolescent Mental Health and Director of the World Health Organization Collaborating Center at Dalhousie University. Yifeng Wei, MEd, is a PhD Candidate at Dalhousie University and School Mental Health Lead of the Sun Life Financial Chair in Adolescent Mental Health Team. The original version of the Guide was developed by Dr. Stan Kutcher in collaboration with the Canadian Mental Health Association (National Office).

TABLE OF CONTENTS

Part 1: Introduction   **4**
     Using the Guide   5
     Reviewing the Guide   9

Part 2: Teacher Knowledge Update   **11**
     Pre/Post Quiz   12
     Pre/Post Quiz Answers   15
     Teacher Knowledge Update   16

Part 3: Student Evaluation   **42**

Part 4: Modules   **50**
     Module 1: The Stigma of Mental Illness   51
     Module 2: Understanding Mental Health and Mental Illness   67
     Module 3: Information on Specific Mental Illnesses   76
     Module 4: Experiences of Mental Illness   108
     Module 5: Seeking Help and Finding Support   113
     Module 6: The Importance of Positive Mental Health   126

Glossary   **140**

Other Resources   **163**

Publications about the Guide   **167**

PART 1: INTRODUCTION

About the Guide

The Mental Health and High School Curriculum Guide (the Guide) is the only evidence based mental health curriculum resource that has been demonstrated to improve both teachers' and students' mental health literacy through usual teacher education and application in the classroom in a variety of program evaluations and research studies in Canada and elsewhere.*

This version of the Guide has replaced the original version, has been rewritten with new materials added and has been updated to reflect Diagnostic and Statistical Manual V (DSM-5) nomenclature. The Guide is now available online with all components found in this book easily accessible using the password found on page 2. The online version of the Guide can be obtained at: **http://teenmentalhealth.org/curriculum/**.

Information about how to access training programs related to the use of the Guide can be found at: **http://teenmentalhealth.org/care/educators/school-mental-health-training-programs/**.

In addition to the online version and supporting materials for the Guide, the website **http://teenmentalhealth.org/** provides a rich repository of materials that can be used by educators and students alike in improving their understanding of mental health and mental disorders.

The Guide has been developed to help enhance the mental health literacy of students and targeted to be used in grades nine and ten (ages 13 to 15 years). This is the time of the lifespan in which the diagnoses of mental disorders begins to increase dramatically; it is thus essential that young people be able to have the knowledge, attitudes and competencies to help themselves and others if necessary. Mental health literacy is defined as having four components:

1) Understanding how to optimize and maintain good mental health

2) Understanding mental disorders and their treatments

3) Decreasing Stigma

4) Enhancing help-seeking efficacy (knowing when and where to get help and having the skills necessary to promote self-care and how to obtain good care)

The Guide helps prepare students for success in each of these domains. Educators using the Guide may wish to use additional information to supplement the resources described in the Guide or to increase their knowledge in youth mental health. While there are many mental health resources available, we recommend two that meet our standards of quality. These are: the handbook "When Something's Wrong: Strategies for Teachers" which can be found at: **http://healthymindscanada.ca/** and the classroom resource "Stop Wondering, Start Knowing" which can be found at: **www.keltymentalhealth.ca.**

*Reports of some of the program evaluations and research on the application of the Guide can be found online at: **http://teenmentalhealth.org/toolbox/.** Publications related to program evaluations and research on the application of the Guide available prior to June 2015 are listed in the section entitled Publications about the Guide (page 166).

PART 1: INTRODUCTION

Using the Guide

This section provides general information about the Guide and suggestions for its classroom application.

Purpose:

The Guide is intended to be used by classroom teachers who have been trained in its application to enhance the mental health literacy of students in grades nine and ten (ages 13 to 15).

Structure:

The Guide consists of both teacher preparation and classroom ready materials that can be easily accessed from the web at **http://teenmentalhealth.org/curriculum/** using the password found on page 2.

The steps to implement the Guide are:

> **Step 1)**   Pre/Post-Quiz
>
> **Step 2)**   Teacher Knowledge Update
>
> **Step 3)**   Student Evaluation
>
> **Step 4)**   Modules

Pre/Post Quiz:

The purpose of this component is to help facilitate self-study for the teacher prior to applying the Guide in the classroom. Taking the Pre-Quiz will help you identify areas in which your knowledge base needs enhancement. After taking the Pre-Quiz, keep a record of those questions that you have answered incorrectly. Then read the Teacher Knowledge Update and pay particular attention to finding the information related to the questions that you answered incorrectly. Upon reading the Teacher Knowledge Update, take the Post-Quiz. If you have answered any questions in the Post-Quiz incorrectly please return to the Teacher Knowledge Update and review the section(s) therein that relate to the questions you answered incorrectly. Once you have answered all Post-Quiz questions correctly please proceed to the Student Evaluation component.

Teacher Knowledge Update:

The purpose of this component is to provide basic information about mental health and mental disorders that will help the teacher better apply the Guide resource in the classroom.

PART 1: INTRODUCTION

Using the Guide (cont.)

Student Evaluation:

The purpose of this component is to provide teachers with a ready-made classroom test that can be used as part or all of their evaluation of their student's learning once the Guide (all modules) have been taught. It includes both knowledge and attitude questions which allow for teacher evaluation of both of these important dimensions of mental health literacy. It can be applied prior to the teaching of the Guide in the classroom and then repeated after the end of Module Six. This evaluation procedure will allow for a robust determination of student learning by comparing scores for each student across pre-and-post-applications. Alternatively, teachers may choose to apply the student evaluation only upon completion of the six modules and not compare pre-and-post-scores.

Modules:

The purpose of this component is to provide teachers with classroom ready lesson plans, activities and easily accessible resources to assist them in applying the Guide. The six modules are designed to be taught in sequence. All modules have two sections: Core Materials and Supplementary Materials. The Core Materials are designed to be used for all students and are required to be taught in the classroom so as to achieve the outcomes identified in the research and evaluation of this resource. The Supplementary Materials are designed for use by students who want to spend additional time and effort to learn more about the module topic. Teachers are encouraged to use their discretion in the introduction of the Supplementary Materials in their classes. Teachers should familiarize themselves with BOTH the Core Materials and Supplementary Materials and decide if and how they will introduce the Supplementary Materials in their classrooms once the Core Materials have been taught.

Format of the modules:

As you review the modules, you will find that each one includes several key features:

- The Overview provides a summary of the module

- The Learning Objectives lists specific understandings or competencies students should derive from completing the modules

- The Major Concepts section presents the central ideas that the module is designed to address

- Teacher Background provides ideas about suggested information that should be reviewed prior to teaching the module to enhance your understanding of the content so that you can confidently facilitate class discussions, answer students' questions and provide additional examples and illustrations

- The Activities section provides details about classroom application

PART 1: INTRODUCTION

Using the Guide (cont.)

- The Required Materials section provides resources needed to complete the activities in each module

- The In Advance section provides instructions for collecting and preparing materials required to complete the activities in the module

- Notes to Teachers appear as sidebars. Look here for information about issues that may need to be emphasized

The Guide and Existing School Curriculum:

The Guide is not meant to replace existing school curriculum. It is meant to be a classroom resource applied by usual classroom teachers that can be used within existing curriculum frameworks to enhance the mental health literacy of both students and teachers. Research on various strategies in classroom application of the Guide has identified that optimal results can be obtained by: training teachers on how to apply the Guide in their classrooms, teaching the Guide as part of a curriculum component (within an appropriate subject area such as Health and Physical Education, Personal Development, Family Studies, etc.) and teaching the Guide as a block (six modules taught consecutively over a period of 8 to 12 hours). The modules were designed to each fit into 60 minutes of classroom time. Based on feedback from teachers and students however, Module Three of the Guide is the longest and most information intense module and may require more teaching time than other modules. We recommend that 1 1/2 to 2, fifty minute blocks be allocated to Module Three.

Resources in the Guide:

The Guide provides the teacher with resources meant to engage the student in her/his learning, be interactive, experiential, to stimulate critical thinking and personal reflection and to help stimulate a search for greater knowledge. This resource includes printed materials, animated videos, PowerPoint presentations and web-downloadable materials. Interactive teaching tips and suggestions for guided discussion are also provided.

Teachers are free to use other resources that they think will be appropriate. However, some resources are more reliable and accurate than others, therefore we have created the "Chair Certified Resource" committee to suggest content valid resources for teachers to use in the classroom. These resources have undergone extensive professional review and are known to be both up-to-date and consistent with best available scientific knowledge. They are periodically updated, and posted on the website. The developers of the Guide do realize that there are other sources of information about mental health and mental disorders available and have identified some credible and trustworthy websites in the section "Further Resources and Information about the Guide". We suggest that teachers use the Guide resources as they appear in each module and supplement these with other materials obtained from those websites that we have identified to ensure as much as possible that valid and appropriate information is used in the classroom.

PART 1: INTRODUCTION

Using the Guide (cont.)

Some of the modules lend themselves to the use of resources from outside the classroom or the school. For example, in-school student services professionals (such as psychologists or social workers) or health and human services professionals from community agencies (such as physicians, psychologists, social workers, substance abuse specialists, etc.) may be able to add invaluable input into what students are learning (for example, in Module Five addressing help-seeking). In some schools, organized speakers from credible organizations (for example, the Canadian Mental Health Organization) may be available to provide additional inputs. Teachers choosing to employ these resources should ensure that the person addressing the class belongs to a responsible and credible organization or institution and that the presenter understands what the goals and expected outcomes of their presentation are meant to be.

PART 1: INTRODUCTION

Reviewing the Guide

Module	Major Concepts
Module 1: The stigma of mental illness	• Stigma acts as a barrier to people seeking help for mental health problems and mental illness. • Learning the facts about mental illness can help dispel misconceptions and stigma. • People's attitudes about mental illness can be positively influenced by exposure to accurate information. • We all have a responsibility to fight the stigma associated with mental illness.
Module 2: Understanding mental health and mental illness	• Everyone has mental health regardless of whether or not they have mental illness. • The brain controls our thinking, perceptions, emotions, physical activities, behaviour and provides us with cues about how to adopt our environment (signaling). • A mental illness is a health condition arising from changes in usual brain functioning that causes that person substantial difficulty in functioning. • Mental illnesses have complex causes that include a biological basis and are therefore not that different from other illnesses. As with all illnesses, the sooner people obtain effective treatment for mental illness, the better their outcomes.
Module 3: Information on specific mental illnesses	• All mental illnesses reflect difficulties in: thinking, perception, emotions, physical activities, behaviour and signaling.

9

PART 1: INTRODUCTION

Reviewing the Guide

Module	Major Concepts
Module 3 (cont.): Information on specific mental illness	• The exact cause of mental illnesses is not yet known, but complex interactions between a person's biology and his/her environment are involved. • Like illnesses that affect other parts of the body, mental illnesses are treatable and the sooner people receive proper treatment and support, the better the outcomes.
Module 4: Experiences of mental illness	• Mental illnesses are diseases that affect many aspects of a person's life. • With appropriate support and treatment, most people with a mental illness can function effectively in everyday life. • Getting help early increases the chances that a person will make a full recovery from mental illness. • Mental illnesses, like physical illnesses, can be effectively treated.
Module 5: Seeking help and finding support	• There are many ways of seeking help for mental health problems and mental illnesses, and resources are available within schools and within the community. • Knowing the signs and symptoms of mental illness helps people know how to distinguish the normal ups and downs of life from something more serious. • Recovery from mental illness is possible, when a range of supports, beyond formal treatment, are available. • Everyone has mental health that can be supported and promoted, regardless of whether or not they also have a mental illness.
Module 6: The importance of positive mental health	• Positive coping strategies can help everyone maintain and enhance their mental health. • There are skills and strategies that we can learn to help us obtain and maintain good mental health.

PART 2: TEACHER KNOWLEDGE UPDATE

Teachers Mental Health Knowledge Update Handbook

This handbook is both part of this Guide resource and available separately on the **www.teenmental-health.org** website at the direct URL: **http://teenmentalhealth.org/toolbox/school-mental-health-teachers-training-guide-english/**.

It is meant to be used by classroom teachers for two purposes. The first purpose is for teachers to study the material in the handbook before they apply the modules in their classrooms so that they can upgrade their knowledge about mental health and mental disorders. The second purpose is that this handbook can be used as a supplementary resource for students to use in Module Three. Teachers can make this easily available to their students either by providing them with the website link or by photocopying the PDF and placing the hard copy in the classroom – or both!

Remember, teachers are using this handbook to support their application of the Guide resource in their classroom teaching. This is being done to improve the mental health literacy of students. This handbook is not to be used to support the delivery of diagnosis or treatment recommendations for students or parents.

The role of the teacher does not include diagnosis or treatment recommendations. It does include teaching of mental health literacy, responding to student's/parent's concerns by supportive listening and referral to the most appropriate person within the school to help address those concerns (such as a counselor, social worker, psychologist) and providing ongoing academically appropriate support to the student as part of the school's integrated response to the student's needs.

Using the Handbook for Self-Study:

> **Step 1:** Before reading the Teacher Knowledge Update, take the self-evaluation Pre-Quiz (30 questions) and answer each question as true or false. Keep a record of the questions for which you provided the wrong answer – to make sure that you cover those areas when you read the Teacher Knowledge Update.

> **Step 2:** Carefully read the Teacher Knowledge Update, paying particular attention to areas in which your Pre-Quiz answers were not correct.

> **Step 3:** Take the Post-Quiz (repeat of the Pre-Quiz). If you have any wrong answers in the Post-Quiz please go back to the relevant section of the Teacher Knowledge Update and make sure you have mastered the material there. Once you have all the answers correct you are ready to proceed to the use of the Guide materials as found in the Modules.

The password needed to access the Modules is: t33nh3alth

Note: The Guide resource has been extensively researched (see page 166 for some recent publications) and has demonstrated significant and substantial positive impacts on improvement in teachers' and students' knowledge and a decrease in stigma. This research however is based on applying a training program for teachers to take prior to applying the Guide resource in their classrooms. If your school, school board, organization or institution would like to obtain that training please contact us at: **info@teenmentalhealth.org**.

PRE/POST QUIZ

1. A phobia is an intense fear about something that might be harmful (such as heights, snakes, etc.)

   a. true   b. false

2. Useful interventions for adolescent mental disorders include BOTH psychological and pharmacologic treatment.

   a. true   b. false

3. Mental distress can occur in someone who has a mental disorder.

   a. true   b. false

4. Stigma against the mentally ill is uncommon in Canada.

   a. true   b. false

5. Substance abuse is commonly paired with a mental disorder.

   a. true   b. false

√6. The most common mental disorders in teenage girls are eating disorders.

   a. true   b. false

7. The stresses of being a teenager are a major factor leading to adolescent suicide.

   a. true   b. false

8. Three of the strongest risk factors for teen suicide are: romantic breakup, conflict with parents, and school failure.

   a. true   b. false

9. Schizophrenia is a split personality.

   a. true   b. false

√10. A depressed mood that lasts for a month or longer in a teenager is very common and should not be confused with a clinical depression that may require professional help.

   a. true   b. false

11. Teen suicide rates have decreased over the last decade in North America.

   a. true   b. false

12. Diet, exercise and establishing a regular sleep cycle are all effective treatments for many mental disorders in teenagers.

    a. true   b. false

13. Anorexia nervosa is very common in teenage girls.

    a. true   b. false

14. Bipolar disorder is another form for manic depressive illness.

    a. true   b. false

✓15. Many clinical depressions that develop in teenagers come "out of the blue".

    a. true   b. false

16. Obsessions are thoughts that are unwanted and known not to be correct.

    a. true   b. false

17. Serotonin is a liver chemical that helps control appetite.

    a. true   b. false

18. Mental disorders may affect between 15-20 percent of Canadians.

    a. true   b. false

19. Most people with panic disorder do not get well with treatment.

    a. true   b. false

20. Depression affects about 2 percent of people in North America.

    a. true   b. false

21. A psychiatrist is a medical doctor who specializes in treating people who have a mental illness.

    a. true   b. false

PRE/POST QUIZ

22. Attention Deficit Hyperactivity Disorder (ADHD) is equally common in boys and girls.

    a. true   b. false

23. A hallucination is defined as a sound that comes from nowhere.

    a. true   b. false

24. Panic disorder is a type of Anxiety disorder.

    a. true   b. false

25. Medications called "anti-psychotics" are helpful to treat the symptoms of Schizophrenia.

    a. true   b. false

26. A delusion is defined as seeing something that is not real.

    a. true   b. false

√ 27. Lack of pleasure, hopelessness and fatigue can all be symptoms of a clinical depression.

    a. true   b. false

28. Nobody with Schizophrenia ever recovers.

    a. true   b. false

29. People with mania may experience strange feelings of grandiosity.

    a. true   b. false

30. Mental disorders are psychological problems caused by poor nutrition.

    a. true   b. false

(See answer key end of this section)

PRE/POST QUIZ ANSWERS

1.	True	16.	True
2.	True	17.	False
3.	True	18.	True
4.	False	19.	False
5.	True	20.	False
6.	False	21.	True
7.	False	22.	False
8.	False	23.	False
9.	False	24.	True
10.	False	25.	True
11.	True	26.	False
12.	False	27.	True
13.	False	28.	False
14.	True	29.	True
15.	True	30.	False

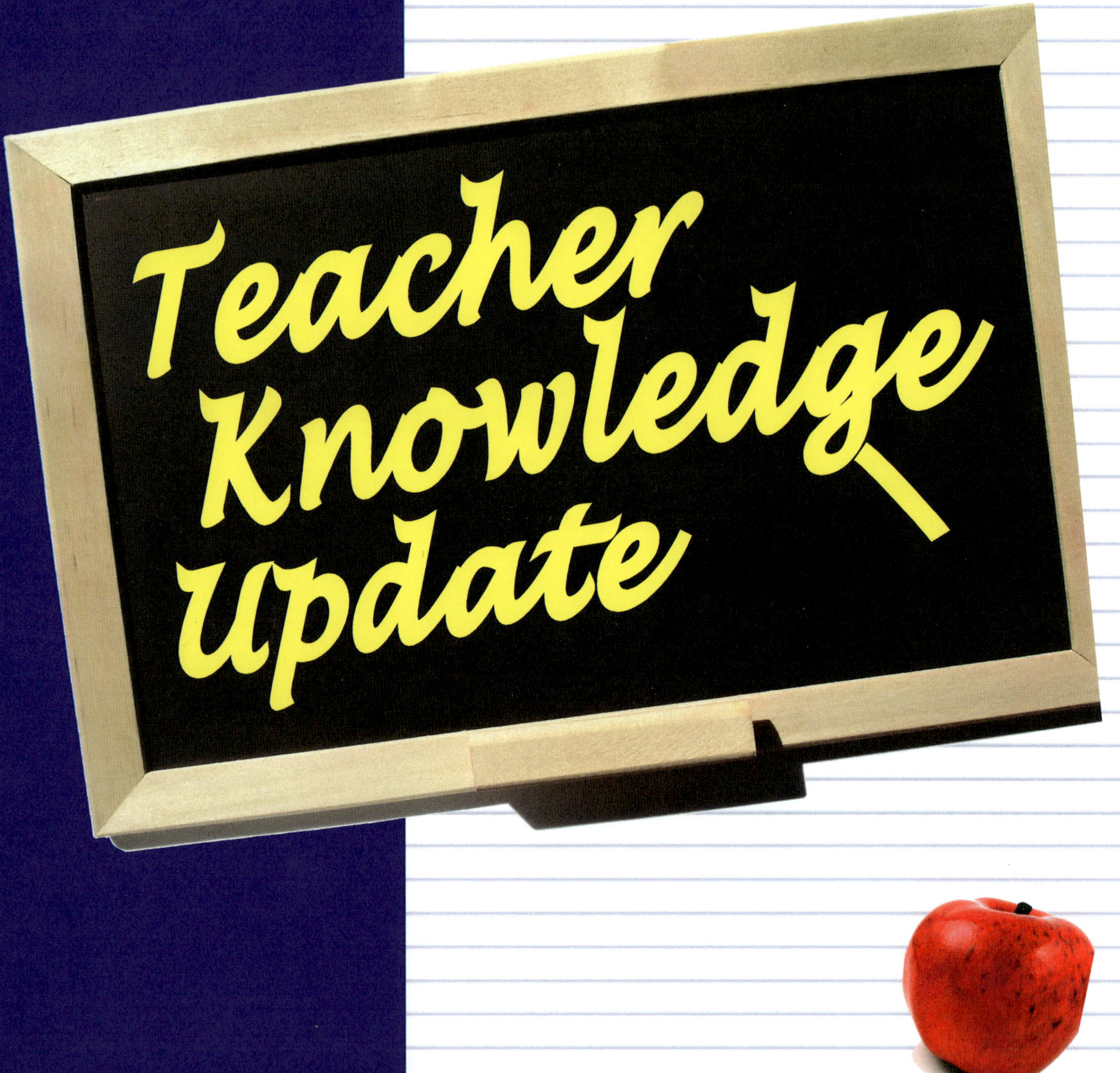

Teacher Knowledge Update

2015 version

teen mental health .org

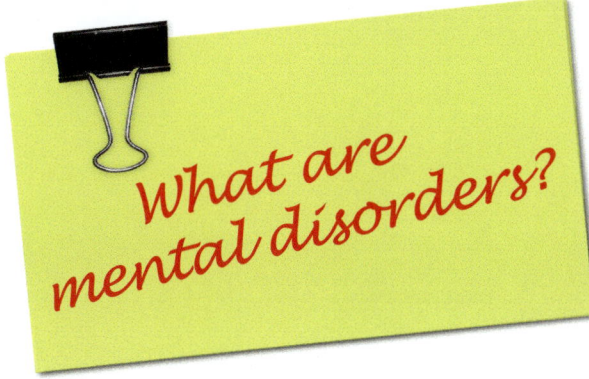

What are mental disorders?

Here's what we know about mental disorders:

• Disturbances of emotion, thinking, and/or behaviour
• May occur spontaneously (without a precipitant)
• Severe (problematic to the individual and others)
• Lead to functional impairment (interpersonal, social)
• Prolonged
• Often require professional intervention
• Derive from brain dysfunctions — brain disorder
• Is rarely, if ever, caused by stress alone

Mental disorders are NOT:

- It is not the consequence of poor parenting or bad behaviour
- It is not the result of personal weakness or deficits in personality
- It is not the manifestation of malevolent spiritual intent
- Only in exceptional cases is it caused by nutritional factors
- It is not caused by poverty

How is the Brain Involved?

- The brain is made up of: cells, connections amongst the cells and various neurochemicals
- The neurochemicals provide a means for the different parts of the brain to communicate
- Different parts of the brain are primarily responsible for doing different things (e.g. movement)
- Most things a brain does depends on many different parts of the brain working together in a network

WHAT HAPPENS INSIDE THE BRAIN WHEN IT GETS SICK?

- A specific part of the brain that needs to be working on a specific task is not working well
- A specific part of the brain that needs to be working on a specific task is working in the wrong way
- The neurochemical messengers that help different parts of the brain communicate are not working properly

HOW DOES THE BRAIN SHOW IT'S NOT WORKING WELL?

- If the brain is not working properly, one or more of its functions will be disturbed
- Disturbed functions that a person directly experiences (such as sadness, sleep problems, etc.) are called SYMPTOMS
- Disturbed functions that another person sees (such as over activity, withdrawal, etc.) are called SIGNS
- BOTH signs and symptoms can be used to determine if the brain may not be working well
- The person's usual life or degree of functioning is also disrupted because of the signs and symptoms

Mental disorders are associated with disturbances in six primary domains of brain function:

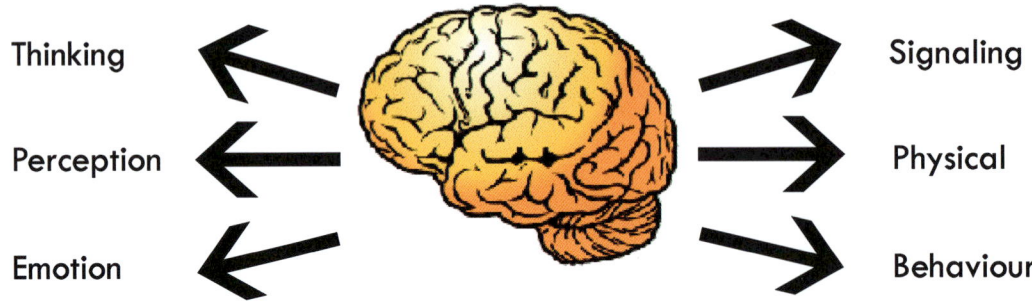

Thinking

Perception

Emotion

Signaling

Physical

Behaviour

When the brain is not functioning properly in one or more of its six domains, and the person experiences problems that interfere with his or her life in a significant way - they may have a mental disorder.

BUT...

Not all disturbances of brain functioning are mental disorders. Some can be a normal or expected response to the environment – for example: grief when somebody dies or acute worry, sleep problems and emotional tension when faced with a natural disaster such as a hurricane.

What's the Difference Between Mental Distress and Mental Disorders?

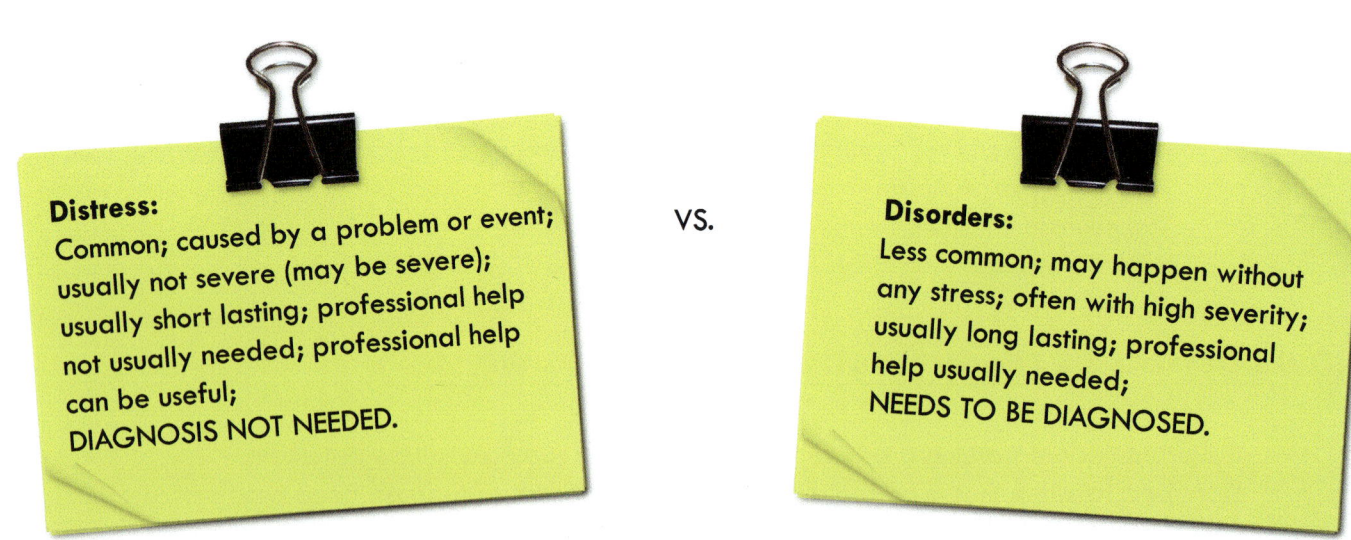

Distress:
Common; caused by a problem or event; usually not severe (may be severe); usually short lasting; professional help not usually needed; professional help can be useful;
DIAGNOSIS NOT NEEDED.

VS.

Disorders:
Less common; may happen without any stress; often with high severity; usually long lasting; professional help usually needed;
NEEDS TO BE DIAGNOSED.

What Causes Mental Illness?

A variety of different influences to the brain can lead to mental illness. Basically there are TWO major causes that can be independent or can interact:

18

GENETICS (the effect of genes on brain development and brain function) and

ENVIRONMENT (the effect of things outside the brain on the brain – such as infection, malnutrition, severe stress, etc.)

Classification of Mental Disorders:

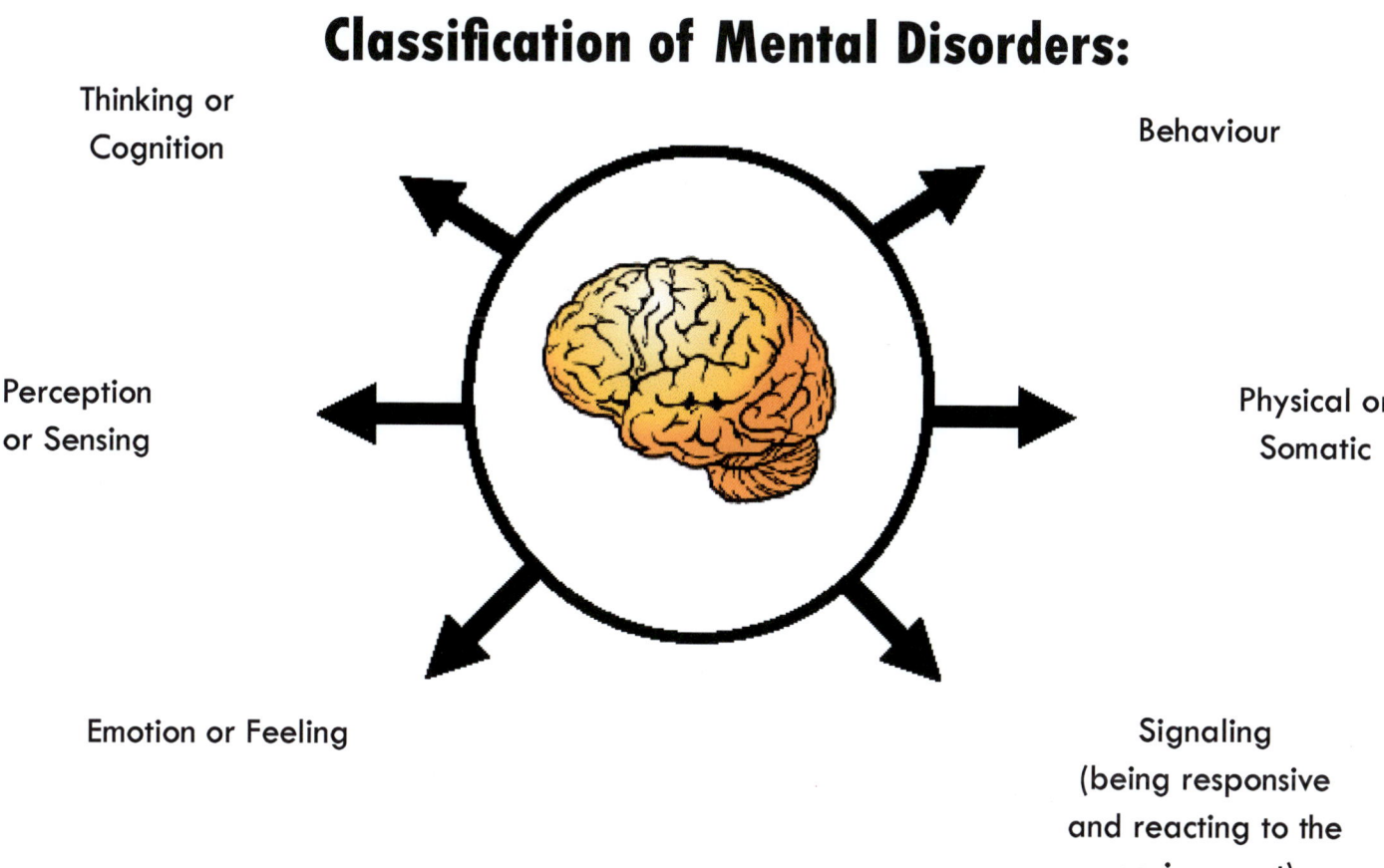

Thinking or Cognition

Behaviour

Perception or Sensing

Physical or Somatic

Emotion or Feeling

Signaling (being responsive and reacting to the environment)

Mental Disorders of Thinking & Cognition: (Psychotic disorders)

WHAT ARE PSYCHOTIC DISORDERS?

Psychotic disorders are a group of illnesses characterized by severe disturbances in the capacity to distinguish between what is real and what is not real. The person with psychosis exhibits major problems in thinking and behaviour. These include symptoms such as delusions and hallucinations. These result in many impairments that significantly interfere *with the capacity to meet ordinary demands of life. Schizophrenia is an example of a psychotic disorder that affects about 1% of the population.*

Who is at risk for developing Schizophrenia?

Schizophrenia (SCZ) often begins in adolescence and there often may be a genetic component although not always. A family history of SCZ, a history of birth trauma and a history of fetal damage in utero increases the risk for SCZ. Significant marijuana use may bring on SCZ in young people who are at higher risk for the illness.

What does Schizophrenia look like?

Delusions are erroneous beliefs that may involve misinterpretation of experiences or perceptions. One common type of delusion is persecutory (also commonly called paranoid) in which the person thinks that he or she is being harmed in some way by another person, force or entity (such as God, the police, spirits, etc.). Strongly held minority religious or cultural beliefs are not delusions.

Hallucinations are perceptions (such as hearing sounds or voices, smelling scents, etc.) that may occur in any sensory modality in the absence of an actual sensory stimulus. They can be normal during times of extreme stress or in sleep like states. Occasionally they can occur spontaneously (such as a person hearing their name called out loud) but these do not cause problems with everyday life and are not persistent.

Thinking is disorganized in form and in content. For example, the pattern of speaking may not make sense to others or what is being said may not make sense or be an expression of delusional ideas.

Behaviour can be disturbed. This can range from behaviours that are mildly socially inappropriate to very disruptive and even threatening behaviours that may be responses to hallucinations or part of a delusion. Self-grooming and self-care may be also compromised.

A young person with Schizophrenia will also demonstrate a variety of cognitive problems ranging from difficulties with concentration to "higher order" difficulties such as with abstract reasoning and problem-solving. Most people with Schizophrenia will also exhibit what are called "negative symptoms" which include: flattening of mood, decreased speech, and lack of will.

A person with Schizophrenia may exhibit delusions, hallucinations and disordered thinking (also called "positive symptoms") as well as negative symptoms at different times during the illness.

What are the criteria for the diagnosis of Schizophrenia?

1 – Positive symptoms as described above (delusions, hallucinations, disorganized thinking)
2 – Negative symptoms as described above
3 – Behavioural disturbances as described above
4 – Significant dysfunction in one or more areas of daily life (social, family, interpersonal, school/work, etc.)
5 – These features must last for at least 6 months during which time there must be at least one month of positive symptoms

What can I do if it is SCZ?

A young person with SCZ will require immediate effective treatment – usually in a specialty mental health program (first onset psychosis program). If an educator suspects SCZ a referral to the most appropriate health provider should be made following discussion with the parents about the concerns.

What do I need to watch out for?

Many young people with SCZ will demonstrate a slow and gradual onset of the illness – often over the period of 6 – 9 months or more. Early signs include: social withdrawal, odd behaviours, lack of attention to personal hygiene, excessive preoccupation with religious or philosophical constructs, etc. Occasionally the young person suffering in the prodrome may exhibit very unusual behaviours – often in response to a delusion or hallucinations. Sometimes it may be difficult to distinguish the onset of SCZ (also called a "prodrome") from other mental disorders – such as Depression or Social Anxiety Disorder. Young people suffering from the prodrome of SCZ may also begin abusing substances – particularly alcohol or marijuana and develop a substance abuse disorder concurrently. Occasionally the young person may share bizarre ideas or may complain about being persecuted by others or may appear to be responding to internal voices. Rarely these delusions or hallucinations may be accompanied by unexpected violent acts.

Questions to ask:

Can you tell me what you are concerned about? Do you feel comfortable in school (your class)? Are you having any problems thinking? Are you hearing or seeing things that others may not be hearing or seeing?

Mental Disorders of Emotion and Feeling: (Mood disorders)

There are two types of mood disorders which include unipolar mood disorders and bipolar mood disorders. Unipolar disorder is major depression, whereas Bipolar Disorder is when a person experiences cycles of Depression and Mania.

DEPRESSION

Not to be confused with the word "depression" which is commonly used to describe emotional distress or sadness, Depression means CLINICAL DEPRESSION, which is a mental disorder.

What are the different types of Depression?

There are two common kinds of clinical depression, Major Depressive Disorder (MDD) and Dysthymic Disorder (DD). Both can significantly and negatively impact on people's lives. They can lead to social, personal and family difficulties as well as poor vocational/educational performance and even premature death due to suicide. Additionally, patients with other illnesses such as heart disease and diabetes have an increased risk of death if they are also diagnosed with Depression. This is thought to be due to the physiological effects that Depression has on your body as well as lifestyle effects such as poor self-care, increased smoking and alcohol consumption. Individuals with clinical depression usually require treatment from health professionals but in mild cases may experience substantial improvement with strong social supports and personal counseling.

What do MDD and DD look like?

MDD is usually a life-long disorder beginning in adolescence or early adulthood and is characterized by periods (lasting months to years) of depressive episodes that are usually self-limiting. The episodes may be separated by periods (lasting months to years) of relative mood stability. Sometimes the depressive episodes may be triggered by a negative event (such as the loss of a loved one, severe and persistent stress such as economic difficulties or conflict) but often the episodes may occur spontaneously. Often there is a family history of Clinical Depression, Alcoholism, Anxiety Disorder or Bipolar Disorder. DD is a low-grade depression that lasts for many years. It is less common than MDD.

What is a depressive episode?

A depressive episode is characterized by three symptom clusters: 1. mood 2. thinking (often called cognitive) and 3. body sensations (often called somatic). MDD may present differently in different cultures, particularly in the somatic problems that people present with. Some symptoms include:
- Must be severe enough to cause functional impairment (stop the person from doing what he or she would otherwise be doing, or decrease the quality of what he/she is doing)
- Must be continuously present every day, most of the day for at least two weeks
- Cannot be due to a substance or medicine or medical illness and must be different from the persons usual state

These symptoms are:

Mood:
• Feeling "depressed", "sad", "unhappy" (or whatever the cultural equivalent of these descriptors is)
• Feeling a loss of pleasure or a marked disinterest in all or almost all activities
• Feelings of worthlessness, hopelessness or excessive and inappropriate guilt
Thinking:
• Diminished ability to think or concentrate or substantial indecisiveness
• Suicidal thoughts/plans or preoccupation with death and dying
Body Sensations:
• Excessive fatigue or loss of energy
• Significant sleep problems (difficulty falling asleep or sleeping excessively)
• Physical slowness or in some cases excessive restlessness
• Significant decrease in appetite that may lead to noticeable weight loss

Criteria:

FIVE of the above symptoms must be present EVERYDAY for MOST OF THE DAY during the same two week period; ONE of the FIVE symptoms MUST BE either depressed mood or loss of interest or pleasure.

What can I do if it is Depression?

You can identify the disorder and counsel the person with the disorder (including education of the person and family) if it is mild and if you are trained in counseling. If the disorder is more intense or the person is suicidal you should immediately refer the person to the health professional best suited to treat the depression. Ideally this should be done in collaboration and with the active support of the school guidance counselor or identified school based mental health provider. Once an intervention occurs and the young person is back at school it is important that you be part of the ongoing treatment team and help develop and address learning needs. You may also need to continue to provide realistic emotional support.

Questions to ask:

Have you lost interest or pleasure in the things that you usually like to do? Have you felt sad, low, down or hopeless? Are you feeling like ending it all? IF the student answers yes to either of these, further assessment of all of the symptoms should be directed to the appropriate health care sector.

Things to look for:

People with depression are at an increased risk for attempting suicide. Every person with depression should be monitored for suicide thoughts and plans. As a teacher you need to be aware that a depressed student who begins to talk about suicide needs to be referred to his/her health provider immediately.

BIPOLAR DISORDER

•Illness is characterized by cycles (episodes) of depression and mania
•   Cycles can be frequent (daily) or infrequent (many years apart)
•   During depressive or manic episodes the person may become psychotic
•   Suicide rates are high in people with bipolar mood disorder

In Bipolar Disorder how is 'mania' different from feeling extremely happy?

- Mood is mostly elevated or irritable
- Many behavioural, physical and thinking, problems
- Significant problems in daily life because of the mood
- Mood may often not reflect the reality of the environment
- Is not caused by a life problem or life event

Bipolar Disorder - what to look for:

- History of at least one depressive episode and at least one manic episode
- Rapid mood changes including irritability and anger outbursts
- Self-destructive or self-harmful behaviours – including: spending sprees, violence towards others, sexual indiscretions, etc.
- Drug or alcohol overuse, misuse or abuse
- Psychotic symptoms including: hallucinations and delusions

Mental Disorder of Signaling: (The Anxiety Disorders)

WHAT IS GENERALIZED ANXIETY DISORDER?

GAD is described as excessive anxiety and worry occurring for an extended period of time about several different things. This persistent apprehension, worry and anxiety causes distress and leads to physical symptoms.

Who is at risk for developing GAD?

GAD often begins in childhood or adolescence and there is also a genetic or familial component. Once GAD is present, the severity can fluctuate and exacerbations often occur during times of stress. Other psychiatric disorders are also risk factors for GAD such as depression, panic disorder and agoraphobia.

What does Generalized Anxiety Disorder look like?

Generalized Anxiety Disorder (GAD) is characterized by excessive anxiety and worry about many different things. The worry is out of proportion to the concern or event. This anxiety and worry must be noticeably greater than the usual socio-cultural norms. Youth with GAD often do not present with panic attacks as in panic disorder. Often they present with physical complaints such as headaches, fatigue, muscle aches and upset stomach. These symptoms tend to be chronic and young people may miss school or social activities because of these physical symptoms.

How do you differentiate GAD from normal worrying?

Anxiety can be broken into four categories:

1) *Emotions* – i.e. feeling fearful, worried, tense or on guard.
2) *Body Responses* – anxiety can cause many different responses of the body including increased heart rate, sweating, and shakiness, shortness of breath, muscle tension and stomach upset.
3) *Thoughts* – when experiencing anxiety, people are more likely to think about things related to real or potential sources of danger and may have difficulty concentrating on anything else. An example is thinking something bad is going to happen to a loved one.
4) *Behaviours* – people may engage in activities that can potentially eliminate the source of the danger. Examples include avoiding feared situations, people or places and self-medicating with drugs or alcohol.

When does anxiety become a disorder?

These physical, emotional and behavioural responses to perceived danger are normal reactions that we experience everyday. Many times this 'anxiety response' is automatic, and every creature has these automatic responses as a way of protecting themselves from danger. However, anxiety becomes a problem when:

- It is greater intensity and/or duration then typically expected given the context
- It leads to impairment or disability in work, school or social environments
- It leads to avoidance of daily activities in an attempt to lessen the anxiety

What are the criteria for the diagnosis of GAD?

1. Excessive anxiety and worry occurring for at least 6 months about several things
2. Difficulty controlling the worry
3. The anxiety and worry are associated with 3 or more of the following:
   a. Restlessness or feeling on edge, fatigued, difficulty concentrating, muscle tension or sleep disturbance
4. Anxiety and worry are not due to substance abuse, a medical condition or a mental disorder
5. The anxiety and physical symptoms cause marked distress and significant impairment in daily functioning

What can I do if it is Generalized Anxiety Disorder?

The first thing is to identify the problem for the young person and elicit assistance from a helper knowledgeable about the problem. Some people with GAD will experience improvements in their anxiety and functioning with supportive cognitive-based counseling. Others may require medication. Referral to an appropriate health professional for medical attention could be considered if the GAD is severe and if the functional impairment is extensive. For some, merely knowing that they have GAD and receiving supportive counseling may be helpful enough.

Questions to ask?

Can you tell me about your worries? Do you or others see you as someone who worries much more than he/she should? Do you or others consider you to be someone who worries much more than most people do? Do you have trouble "letting go of the worries"? Do you sometimes feel sick with worry — in what way? What things that you enjoy doing or would like to do are made less enjoyable or are avoided because of the worries? What if anything do you find makes the worries better — is this for a short or a long time?

SOCIAL PHOBIA

What is Social Phobia?

Social Phobia, also known as Social Anxiety Disorder, is characterized by the presence of an intense fear of scrutiny by others, which may result in embarrassment or humiliation.

What does Social Phobia look like?

Young people with social phobia fear doing something humiliating in front of others, or of offending others. They fear that others will judge everything they do in a negative way. They believe they may be considered to be flawed or worthless if any sign of poor performance is detected. They may cope by trying to do everything perfectly, limiting what they are doing in front of others and gradually withdraw from contact with others. Youth with Social Phobia often experience panic symptoms in social situations. As a result they tend to avoid social situations such as parties or school events. Some may have a difficult time attending class or may avoid going to school altogether. Although young people with Social Phobia recognize that their fears are excessive and irrational, they are unable to control it and therefore avoid situations that trigger their anxiety. The presentation of Social Phobia may vary across cultures and although it may occur in children it usually onsets in the adolescent years. It must not be confused with "shyness" and the strength of the fears may wax and wane over time.

Things to look for:

Some people with GAD may go on to develop a clinical depression. Some people may begin to use substances such as alcohol to help control their anxiety. If this occurs, they may be at risk of developing a substance abuse or substance dependence problem.

What are the criteria for diagnosis of Social Phobia?

The following must be present for someone to have Social Phobia:

• Marked and persistent fear of social or performance situations in which the person is exposed to unfamiliar people; fear of embarrassment or humiliation

• Exposure to the feared situation almost always provokes marked anxiety or panic

• The person recognizes that the fear is excessive or inappropriate

• The avoidance or fear causes significant impairment in functioning and distress

25

- The feared social or performance situations are avoided or else endured with intense anxiety or distress
- The symptoms are not due to a substance, medicine or general medical condition

In children, Social Phobia may be expressed by crying, tantrums, and a variety of clingy behaviours. Other psychiatric diagnoses that Social Phobia must be differentiated from include: Panic Disorder, Pervasive Developmental Disorder, and Schizoid Personality Disorder.

What can I do if it is Social Phobia?

The first step is the identification of the problem. Often, people with Social Phobia will have suffered for many years without knowing the reason for their difficulties. Sometimes just informing and educating them about the problem can be helpful, particularly in mild cases. Treatment is not indicated unless the problem is causing significant functional impairment but counseling using cognitive behavioural techniques and exposure to the anxiety-provoking situation in the company of a counselor may help the person better deal with their difficulties. If the disorder is severe, referral to an appropriate healthcare provider is indicated, and the counselor can provide ongoing support. A teacher may be able to assist in behaviour modification programs (such as getting used to a classroom situation). If you think a student may have Social Phobia it is important not to draw attention publically to their difficulties but speak with them in private about what you notice – be supportive.

What do I need to watch out for?

Some young people with Social Phobia will use excessive amounts of alcohol to help decrease their anxiety in social situations. In some cases, Social Phobia can be a risk factor for the abuse of alcohol or other substances. In young children it is important to differentiate Social Phobia from Pervasive Developmental Disorders such as Autism. Children with autism, in contrast to children with Social Phobia, will not demonstrate age-appropriate social relationships with family members or other familiar people.

Questions to ask

Do situations that are new or associated with unfamiliar people cause you to feel anxious, distressed or panicky? When you are in unfamiliar social situations are you afraid of feeling embarrassed? What kinds of situations cause you to feel that way? Do those feelings of embarrassment, anxiety, distress or panic stop you from doing things you would otherwise do? What have you not been able to do as well as you would like to do because of those difficulties?

WHAT IS PANIC DISORDER?

Panic Disorder is characterized by recurrent, unexpected, anxiety (panic) attacks that involve triggering a number of frightening physical reactions. The frequency and severity of panic attacks can vary greatly and can lead to agoraphobia (fear of being in places in which escape is difficult).

Who is at risk for developing Panic Disorder?

The onset of Panic Disorder is commonly between the ages of 15-25. People who have first-degree relatives with Panic Disorder have an 8x higher risk of also developing Panic Disorder themselves. Panic Disorder is associated with an area of the brain that regulates alertness. Disturbance in this area of the brain is one explanation for why panic attacks occur.

What does Panic Disorder look like?

Young people with Panic Disorder experience recurrent, unexpected panic attacks and they greatly fear having another attack. They persistently worry about having another attack as well as the consequences of having a panic attack. Some may fear they are 'losing their mind' or feel they are going to die. Often they will change their behaviour to avoid places or situations that they fear might trigger a panic attack. In time, the person may come to avoid so many situations that they become bound to their home.

What are the components of a panic attack?

The person has four of more of the following symptoms which peak within 10 minutes:
1. Palpitations, pounding heart or accelerated heart rate
2. Sweating
3. Trembling or shaking
4. Sensations of shortness of breath or smothering
5. Feeling of choking

6. Chest pain or discomfort
7. Nausea or abdominal pain
8. Feeling dizzy, unsteady, lightheaded or faint
9. Feeling of unreality or being detached from oneself
10. Fear of losing control or going crazy
11. Fear of dying
12. Numbness or tingling in the body
13. Chills or hot flashes

What are the criteria for Panic Disorder?

Assessing Panic Disorder involves evaluating 5 areas:
1. Panic attacks
2. Anticipatory anxiety
3. Panic related phobic avoidance
4. Overall illness severity
5. Psychosocial disability

For a diagnosis of Panic Disorder, a patient must have:
1. Recurrent unexpected panic attacks
2. One or more of the attacks has been followed by ≥ 1 month of:
    - Persistent concern of having additional attacks
    - Worry about the implications of the attack or its consequences
    - A significant change in behaviour as a result of the attacks
3. Can be $\pm$ agoraphobia
4. Panic attacks are not due to substance abuse, medications or a general medical condition
5. Panic attacks are not better accounted for by another mental disorder

What can I do if it is a Panic Attack?

The first thing is to identify the panic attack and provide a calm and supportive environment until the attack passes. Education about panic attacks and panic disorder is often very helpful and should ideally be provided by a professional with good knowledge in this area.

Counseling using cognitive behavioural methods may be of help and medications can be used as well. The teacher's role in helping a young person suffering from a panic disorder can also involve assisting them in dealing with their anxieties about having another attack and also helping them with strategies to combat avoidance of social situations. Therefore it is a good idea for a teacher to be part of the treatment planning and treatment monitoring for a youth with panic disorder.

Questions to ask?

Can you describe in your own words what happens when you have one of these episodes (some people will refer to them as "spells")? How many of these episodes have you had in the last week? In the last month? What do these episodes mean to you? What do these episodes stop you from doing that you would otherwise usually do? What do you do when these episodes occur? Do you ever feel that you would like to be dead or think that your problem is so great that you should kill yourself? How do your family, friends, loved ones, etc. react to these episodes? What do they say is the problem?

OBSESSIVE COMPULSIVE DISORDER

Obsessive Compulsive Disorder (OCD) is an anxiety disorder characterized by obsessions and/or compulsions. Obsessions are persistent, intrusive, unwanted thoughts, images or impulses that the person recognizes as irrational, senseless, intrusive or inappropriate but is unable to control. Compulsions are repetitive behaviours, which the person performs in order to reduce anxiety associated with an obsession. Examples of these are counting, touching, washing and checking. Both can be of such intensity that they cause a great deal of distress and significantly interfere with the person's daily functioning. Obsessions are different from psychotic thoughts because the person knows that they are their own thoughts (not put inside their head by some external force) and the person does not want to have the thoughts.

Compulsions are different from psychotic behaviours because the person knows why he/she is doing the activity and can usually say why they are doing them.

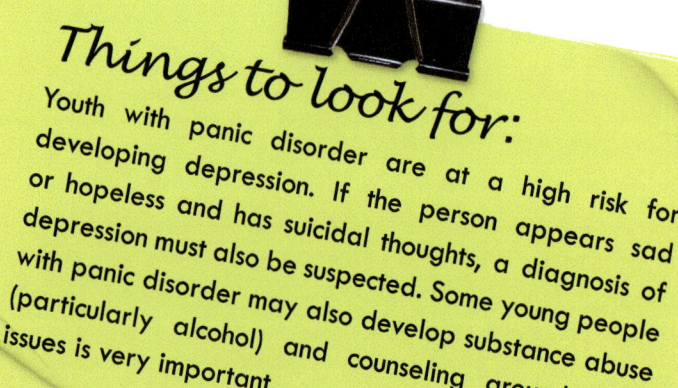

Things to look for:
Youth with panic disorder are at a high risk for developing depression. If the person appears sad or hopeless and has suicidal thoughts, a diagnosis of depression must also be suspected. Some young people with panic disorder may also develop substance abuse (particularly alcohol) and counseling around these issues is very important.

Who is at risk for developing OCD?

OCD often begins in adolescence or early adulthood, although it can start in childhood. It is quite common and affects both men and women. First-degree relatives of people with OCD are more likely to develop OCD. It is important to note that people with OCD are at a higher risk for developing depression and other anxiety disorders.

What does OCD look like?

OCD should not be confused with superstitions or those repetitive checking behaviours that are common in everyday life. They are not simply excessive worries about real life issues. A person with OCD will have significant symptoms of either obsessions or compulsions or both. These symptoms will be severe enough to cause marked distress, are time consuming (take up more than one hour per day) and significantly interfere with a person's normal activities (work, school, social, family, etc.).

Obsessions:
- Recurrent and persistent thoughts, impulses or images that are experienced as intrusive and not appropriate and cause significant distress or anxiety
- These symptoms cannot be simply excessive worries about everyday life
- The person with these symptoms tries to suppress or ignore them. The person may try to neutralize, decrease or suppress the thoughts with some other thought or action.
- The person knows that the thoughts are coming from his/her own mind

Compulsions:
- Repetitive behaviours (such as checking, washing, ordering) or mental acts (such as counting, praying, repeating words silently) that the person feels driven to perform in response to an obsession or according to rigid rules
- These behaviours or mental acts are aimed at preventing or reducing distress or preventing some dreaded event or situation BUT are not realistically connected to the obsessions they are meant to neutralize

How do you differentiate between OCD and Psychosis?

This is a very important step to take if you suspect someone has OCD. In general, patients with OCD have insight into the senselessness of their thoughts and actions and often try to hide their symptoms. This distinguishes OCD from psychotic disorders such as Schizophrenia because those patients lack any insight into the senseless nature of their symptoms.

What can I do if it is OCD?

You can educate the student about OCD and how it is treated. If the symptoms are associated with impairment (social or academic) you should send the student to the school guidance or health professional who can then refer the person to the professional best suited to provide treatment and you can continue to provide education and support to the student if that is mutually agreed to. Often young people will be treated with cognitive behavioural therapy (CBT). Sometimes this may require a teacher's input. It is important to know if any academic modifications need to be made to enhance learning opportunities for young people with OCD so including the teacher in treatment planning and treatment monitoring is usually necessary.

Questions to ask:

Are you having thoughts that are coming into your mind that you do not want to be there? Can you tell me what those thought are? Do those thoughts cause you to feel uncomfortable or anxious or upset? Do you think that those thoughts are true? Where do you think those thoughts are coming from? How are you trying to deal with or stop the thoughts from coming? What do the thoughts stop you from doing that you would otherwise be doing? How much of the time are those thoughts on your mind?

Please describe the things that you are doing that are causing distress to you or other people. Can you tell me why you are doing those things? What do you think will happen if you do not do those things? What do those things that you are doing stop you from doing that you would otherwise be doing? How much time do you spend doing those rituals?

WHAT IS POST TRAUMATIC STRESS DISORDER?

Post Traumatic Stress disorder (PTSD) develops after a trauma occurs that was either experienced or witnessed by the young person. It involves the development of psychological reactions related to the experience such as recurrent, intrusive and distressing recollections of the event. These may be in the form of nightmares, flashbacks and/or hallucinations.

Who is at risk for developing PTSD?

Not all people who have experienced a traumatic event will develop PTSD. Indeed, most will not. Risk factors include personal or family history of depression or anxiety, severity of the trauma and early separation from parents.

What does PTSD look like?

The symptoms of PTSD develop within 6 months following the traumatic event and are organized into three categories:

Things to look for:
There are two main things to watch out for. The first is the possibility that the symptoms could be part of a psychosis. Therefore it is very important to rule out a psychosis disorder. The second thing to watch for is the effect OCD has on the young person's classmates. Sometimes students with severe OCD will try to involve their classmates (or their teachers) in their compulsions. If this happens then it can cause significant problems at school. Educating yourself about OCD and the importance of not participating in the OCD rituals important.

Re-experiencing Symptoms – recurrent, intrusive, distressing recollections or memories of the event in the form of memories, dreams, or flashbacks in which the individual perceives himself/herself to be re-living the event as though it was actually happening again in the present.

Avoidance & Numbing Symptoms – avoidance of anything – people, places, topics of conversation, food, drink, weather conditions, clothing, activities, situations, thoughts, feelings – that are associated with or are reminders of the traumatic event. In addition the person may experience a general numbing of emotions, a loss of interest in previously enjoyed activities, detachment from family and friends, and a sense of hopelessness about the future.

Hyperarousal Symptoms – sleep problems (difficulties falling asleep or staying asleep), irritability, angry outbursts, hypervigilance, exaggerated startle response, and difficulty concentrating.

What are the criteria for the diagnosis of PTSD?

1. The person has been exposed to a traumatic event in which both of the following were present:
   a. The person felt their life was in danger or witnessed someone else's life put in danger
   b. The person experienced extreme fear, helplessness or horror
2. The traumatic event is re-experienced, including one or more of:
   a. Recurrent intrusive memories, dreams or nightmares reliving the event which causes psychological distress.
3. Avoidance of things associated with the event including 3 or more of:
   a. Avoid thoughts, feelings or conversations, avoid activities, places or people, inability to recall aspect of the trauma, decreased interest or participation in activities, feeling detached or estranged from others, restricted range of affect, sense of foreshortened future.
4. Persistent symptoms of increased arousal including 2 or more of:
   a. Difficulty falling or staying asleep, irritability, difficulty concentrating, hypervigilance, exaggerated startle response
5. Duration of symptoms greater than 1 month:
   a. Severity of symptoms causes marked distress and impairment in daily functioning.

How does PTSD differ from Acute Stress Disorder or normal grieving?

PTSD must be distinguished from normal responses (such as grief, distress) to such situations and from Acute Stress Disorder (ASD). ASD has similar symptoms to PTSD but ends or is diminished greatly usually without formal treatment within four weeks of the traumatic event. Duration and severity of PTSD symptoms may vary over time with complete recovery occurring within half a year (or less) in half or more cases.

What can I do if it is PTSD?

The first thing is to identify the young person with PTSD and help them find a knowledgeable helper who can provide education to them about what the problem is and how it can be treated. It is important not to confuse PTSD with normal responses to traumatic events or with ASD. Do not create pathology where it does not exist! For people with PTSD, supportive counseling using cognitive therapy methods may be of help. If the disorder is causing significant distress and impairment, referral to an appropriate health care provider is indicated, as medication may be needed.

What questions can I ask?

Are you bothered by memories or thoughts of a very upsetting event that has happened to you? Make sure that you ask about frequency and persistence of symptoms and include clear evidence of functional impairment before considering PTSD.

Mental Disorder of Physical: (Eating Disorders)

WHAT IS AN EATING DISORDER?

There are two main types of eating disorders – Anorexia Nervosa and Bulimia Nervosa. While there may be some overlapping in symptoms between the two, they are likely to have different causes and the treatments for them differ.

Who is at risk for developing an eating disorder?

Eating disorders usually begin in adolescence and may continue into adulthood. Girls are much more commonly affected than boys.

What does Anorexia Nervosa look like?

Anorexia Nervosa (AN) is characterized by excessive preoccupation with body weight control, a disturbed body image, an intense fear of gaining weight and a refusal to maintain a minimally normal weight. Post-pubertal girls also experience a loss of menstrual periods. There are two subtypes of AN – a restricting subtype (in which the young person does not regularly binge or abuse laxative or self-induce vomiting) and a binge-eating/purging subtype (in which the young person regularly binges and abuses laxatives or self-induces vomiting).

What does Bulimia Nervosa look like?

Bulimia Nervosa (BN) is characterized by regular and recurrent binge-eating (large amounts of food over a short time accompanied by a lack of control over the eating during the episode) and by frequent

and inappropriate behaviours designed to prevent weight gain (including but not limited to: self-induced vomiting, use of laxatives, enemas, excessive exercise).

How do you differentiate an eating disorder from normal teenage eating?

Eating patterns in young people can be very erratic. Food fads are common as are periods of dieting and food

Things to look for:

Some people who are exposed to significantly traumatic events may have exacerbations of pre-existing mental health problems such as anxiety, depression or psychosis. Identification and proper effective interventions for these people in the post traumatic situation is important. Substance abuse, especially involving alcohol is very common in people who have PTSD. Therefore it is important to screen for this problem in people with PTSD and to treat appropriately.

restriction (often in response to concerns about weight). Adolescence is also a period in which some young people experiment with food types and eating experiments that may differ substantially from those common to their families or communities. These are not eating disorders.

What are the criteria for the diagnosis of AN?

1 – Refusal to maintain body weight at or above a minimally normal weight for age and height resulting in a body weight less than 85% of that expected.

2 – Intense fear of gaining weight or becoming fat while underweight.

3 – Substantial disturbances in body image (considers self to be fat even though is underweight) or denial of seriousness of current low body weight.

4 – Loss of menstrual periods in post-pubertal girls.

The prevalence of AN is about 0.2 – 0.5 percent.

What can I do if it is AN?

Young people with AN do not complain about having AN and most deny that they have a problem with being underweight. Usually a friend, teacher or family member will notice the severe weight loss. An educator who is concerned that a student may have AN should gently and supportively discuss the issue with the young person and if after that discussion it seems as if there is a possibility of AN, the young person should be referred to the appropriate support person or health provider in the school for further assessment and intervention. Suggestions that the young person eat more or negative comments on the youth's weight are counterproductive.

What are the criteria for the diagnosis of BN?

1 – Recurrent episodes of binge-eating where both of the following are present: a) – eating large amounts of food in a short period of time; b) – feeling that eating is out of control.

2 – Recurrent inappropriate behaviours in order to control weight (such as: self-induced vomiting; misuse of laxative, diuretics, enemas or other medications, fasting or excessive exercise.)

3 – The above must occur an average at least twice a week for a period of 3 months.

4 – Self perspective is overly influenced by body shape and weight.

5 – The above does not occur exclusively during AN.

There are two subtypes of BN – the purging type (characterized by self-induced vomiting or misuse of laxative, diuretics, enemas, etc.); the non-purging type (no use of the above).

The prevalence of BN is about 1 – 3 percent.

What can I do if it is BN?

Young people with BN do not complain about having BN and most deny that they have a problem with eating. BN is often hidden. Classroom discussions about BN and other eating problems should be undertaken with the sensitivity that there may be a young person with unknown or unrecognized BN in the group.

Questions to ask:

How do you feel about yourself? Has anyone asked you if you were having problems with your eating? Do you sometimes feel that your eating may be out of control?

Mental Disorders of Behaviour:
(ADHD, Substance Abuse, Conduct Disorder)

SUBSTANCE DEPENDENCE AND ABUSE

There is a spectrum of harm that can develop from using various substances. Along this spectrum of harm is abuse and dependence.

What is Substance Abuse?

The abuse of substances is a maladaptive pattern of substance use leading to clinically significant impairment or distress, as manifested by one (or more) of the following, occurring within a 12-month period:

1. Recurrent substance use resulting in a failure to fulfill major role obligations at work, school, or home (e.g., repeated absences or poor work performance related to substance use, substance-related absences, suspensions or expulsions from school, neglect of children or household)
2. Recurrent substance use in situations in which it is physically hazardous (e.g. driving an

Things to look for:
Some people with AN may go on to develop a clinical depression. or severe medical problems. Some young people may begin to avoid class or other school activities. Frequently, young people with AN will avoid eating at times all other young people are eating (such as lunch time in the school cafeteria).

automobile or operating a machine when impaired by substance use)
3. Recurrent substance-related legal problems (e.g. arrests for substance-related disorderly conduct)
4. Continued substance use despite having persistent or recurrent social or interpersonal problems caused or exacerbated by the effects of the substance (e.g. arguments with spouse about consequences of intoxication, physical fights)

What is Substance Dependence?

Substance dependence is a maladaptive pattern of substance use, leading to clinically significant impairment or distress, as manifested by three (or more) of the following, occurring at any time in the same 12-month period:

1. Tolerance, as defined by either of the following:
    *   A need for markedly increased amounts of the substance to achieve intoxication or desired effect.
    *   Markedly diminished effect with continued use of the same amount of substance.

34

2. Withdrawal, as manifested by either of the following:
   - the characteristic withdrawal syndrome for the substance.
   - the same (or a closely related) substance is taken to relieve or avoid withdrawal symptoms.
3. The substance is often taken in larger amounts or over a longer period than was intended.
4. There is a persistent desire or unsuccessful efforts to cut down or control substance use.
5. A great deal of time is spent in activities to obtain the substance, use the substance, or recover from its effects.
6. Important social, occupational or recreational activities are given up or reduced because of substance use.
7. The substance use is continued despite knowledge of having a persistent or recurrent physical or psychological problem that is likely to have been caused or exacerbated by the substance (e.g., continued drinking despite recognition that an ulcer was made worse by alcohol consumption).

Things to look for:
Some people with BN may go on to develop a clinical depression or substance abuse (including excessive amounts of appetite suppressants).

What are types of substances that can be abused?

...use of substances includes those that are legal and illegal. The definition of a drug as a legal or illegal substance does not determine if the substance can induce dependence or abuse. Substances include such things as alcohol, nicotine, cannabis, amphetamines, cocaine, inhalants, opioids, hypnotics and others.

A variety of substances can be safely used in moderation by most people as social modifiers (for example, beer or other alcohol taken with meals or in social situations). Substances which may be abused in some situations can be therapeutic in others – for example, heroin or cocaine can be used to treat pain under medical supervision but are also well known to be addictive substances when used for non-medical purposes.

What can I do if it is Substance Abuse/Dependence?

First, it is important to identify the problem. In some situations, cultural, social or economic factors may impede the identification of the substance problem. The person with the problem will often deny the problem exists and sometimes the person's family or loved ones will also deny that the problem exists. Young people often proceed though a path of substance misuse for a long time (years) before some of them go on to abuse. Most young people who misuse substances likely do not go on to abuse them – therefore substance misuse, although a risk factor for substance abuse is not necessarily predictive of substance abuse. Academic and social problems characterize the young person who suffers from substance abuse – failing grades, missing classes, Monday morning absences, aggression, etc.

Questions to ask:

Try to determine the amounts of the substance used – remember that use can be continuous (for example: daily) or in binge patterns (large amounts used sporadically – such as every three to five days). Determine if the young persons problems are due in whole or in part to excessive use of substances. One particularly important question is "How does taking (name of substance here) help you or hinder you in your school and social life?"

Substance abuse/dependence in young people usually requires professional intervention. Issues such as confidentiality will often arise so it is important that teachers understand what the expectations and limits to confidentiality regarding substance abuse/dependence are in their setting.

Often the advice of a teacher or coach is an important step towards treatment for a young person abusing substances. Non-judgemental but realistic advice from a teacher can sometimes lead them to the realization that they need help. Some young people traffic in the substances that they use. The teacher therefore needs to know the school policy on drugs and abide by it.

What is Attention Deficit Hyperactivity Disorder?

Attention Deficit Hyperactivity Disorder (ADHD) is characterized by a persistent pattern of hyperactivity, impulsivity and substantial difficulties with sustained attention that is outside the population norm and is associated with substantial functional impairments at school, home and with peers. This disorder begins before age seven and continues into adolescence or for some people, even into adulthood.

Who is at risk for ADHD?

ADHD has a genetic component and runs in many families and is more common in boys than in girls. Girls who have ADHD often do not have similar problems with hyperactivity although they have similar problems with sustaining attention. Young people who have learning disabilities and youth with Tourette's Syndrome have higher rates of ADHD. Young people with Conduct Disorder may have ADHD which has not been recognized or treated and which may contribute to their social and legal difficulties.

What does ADHD look like?

Problems with sustaining attention may result in substantial difficulties in on-task behaviours. Young people with ADHD frequently make multiple careless errors, do not complete their academic or house tasks and may start numerous activities. They are easily distracted by stimuli in their environment (such as noises) and often will begin to avoid tasks that require significant attention (such as housework). Young people with ADHD will often rush into things such as games or other activities without taking the time to learn the rules or determine what they should do.

Hyperactivity is often manifested by difficulties staying still in one place — such as sitting at a desk or in a group. Younger children may run around the room (or climb on furniture, etc.) instead of focusing on group activities. Most young people with ADHD have trouble sitting still and are very active — often they will fidget, talk excessively, make noises during quiet activity and generally seem 'wound up' or 'driven'.

Impulsivity is often shown as impatience or low frustration tolerance. Young people with ADHD will often interrupt others, fail to listen to instructions, rush into novel situations without thinking about the consequences, etc. This type of behaviour may lead to accidents. Many youth with ADHD also do not seem to be able to learn from negative experiences — it is as if the impulsivity overrides learning about dangers.

These difficulties can be less pronounced in activities that require a great deal of physical participation and are constantly engaging. Sometimes young people with ADHD seem less distracted when they are playing games that they like —especially games that do not require sustained attention (such as video games). Symptoms are more likely to be noticed when the young person is in a group setting in which sustained and quiet attention is needed or when he/she is working in an environment in which there are many distractions.

Things to look for:

Some people with Substance Dependence/Abuse will also have other mental health problems such as Depression or Anxiety. If these problems occur they should be identified and help for them provided. Suicide may occur more frequently in people with substance problems. Youth who suffer from untreated or inadequately treated ADHD are at higher risk for Substance Abuse. Effective medication treatment of ADHD decreases the risk for Substance Abuse.

What are the criteria for diagnosis of ADHD?

There must be a number of symptoms from each of the following categories: inattention, hyperactivity, impulsivity, PLUS a duration of at least six months to a degree that the person demonstrates maladaptive behaviours and trouble functioning that is inconsistent with their level of development.

Inattention (at least six of the following)

1- Failure to give close attention or many careless errors in work requiring sustained attention (such as school work)

2 - Difficulty sustaining attention in tasks or play

3 - Does not seem to listen when spoken to directly

4 - Does not follow through on instructions

5 - Has difficulty organizing tasks and activities

6 - Avoids tasks that require sustained attention (such as homework)

7 - Loses things needed for tasks and activities

8 - Easily distracted by the environment

9 - Forgetful in daily activities

Hyperactivity

1 - Fidgets or squirms while seated

2 - Leaves seat in classroom or when is supposed to be seated

3 - Runs about or climbs excessively when not appropriate

4 - Has difficulty in solitary play or quiet activities

5 - Is usually on the go, as if motor driven

6 - Often talks excessively

Impulsivity (are included in the number of symptoms for hyperactivity)

7 - Blurts out comments or answers to questions before he/she should

8 - Has difficulty waiting for his/her turn

9 - Often interrupts or intrudes on others

What can I do if it is ADHD?

ADHD can be treated with a combination of medications and other assistance — such as social skills training and cognitive behavioural therapy. The most effective treatment for symptoms is medication. Because learning difficulties are common, young people with ADHD should undergo educational testing to determine if their learning disability is present. Sometimes youth with ADHD will benefit from modifications to their learning environments such as having quieter places in which to work or having homework done in small amounts over long periods of time.

Some young people with ADHD will develop conduct disturbances or substance abuse. Many will become demoralized because of constant reminders from teachers, parents and others about their 'bad behaviour'. Remember that these young people are not bad - they simply have difficulties with sustained attention. Try not to decrease their self-esteem by focusing only on what they have difficulty doing - focus on their strengths as well.

Questions to ask?

Are you having difficulties focusing on your schoolwork? Is it hard for you to finish your work if there are noises or distractions? Do your parents or teachers seem to be nagging you all the time to do your work and sit still?

What is suicide?

Suicide the act of ending one's life. Suicide itself is not a mental disorder but one of the most important causes of suicide is mental illness — most often Depression, Bipolar Disorder (Manic Depression), Schizophrenia, and Substance Abuse.

Suicide is found in every culture and may be the result of complex social, cultural, religious and socio-economic factors in addition to mental disorders. The reasons for suicide may vary from region to region because of these factors. It is therefore important to know what the most common reasons for suicide are in the region in which you are working. This may be difficult to determine accurately because of the "taboos" and stigma around suicide.

The preferred methods of completing suicide may vary from location to location — ranging from firearms to fertilizer poisoning to self-burning to overdosing on pills. Therefore, it is also important to know the most common methods of suicide in the region in which you are working.

What does suicide look like?

Not all self-harm behaviours are attempts to commit suicide. There may be many reasons for self-harm behaviours besides suicide. These include a person attempting to cry for help - for example, from a person who is stuck in a harmful situation that they cannot escape such as ongoing sexual abuse. Certain types of personality disorders can cause youth to perform self-harm behaviors. A suicide attempt is distinguished from a self-harm behavior by the person's intent to die.

Suicidal behavior has three components: ideation, intent, and plans.
1. Suicidal ideation includes ideas about death or dying, wishing that he/she were dead, or ideas about committing suicide. These ideas are not persistent. These ideas can be fairly common in people with mental disorders or in people who are in difficult life circumstances. Most people with suicidal ideation do not go on to commit suicide but the suicidal ideation is a risk factor for suicide.
2. The second component is suicidal intent. With suicidal intent, the idea of committing suicide is better formed and more consistently held than in suicidal ideation. A person with suicidal intent may think about committing suicide most of the time, imaging what life would be like for friends and family without him/her, etc. The strongest intent occurs when the person decides that she/he will commit suicide.

38

3. The third component is the suicide plan. This is a clear plan of how the act of suicide will occur. Vague plans (such as "someday I will jump off a bridge") are considered as part of intent. In a suicide plan the means of committing suicide will be identified and obtained (such a gun, poison, etc.) and the place and time will be chosen. The presence of a suicide plan constitutes a psychiatric emergency.

What can I do if it is Suicide?

The first thing is to identify the presence of suicide ideation, intent and plans. Young people who have thoughts of suicide ideation or have intents may benefit from supportive or cognitive based counseling. The presence of a suicide plan should lead to placement of the person in a situation in which he/she can be safe and secure. That situation should be therapeutic and not punitive and should be accompanied by supportive and cognitive counseling. The family or loved ones may require support and help as well. Non-judgmental supportive counseling may be of assistance in such situation. If a suicide has happened, the family or loved ones may benefit from non-judgmental supportive bereavement counseling.

If a teacher is faced with a student who is talking about or writing about suicide then it is important to include an educator from guidance or health to assess the situation. Generally it is better to err on the side of caution and take the young person to a location in which they can be safe. Schools should have policies about how to deal with a suicidal youth – know your school's policy. If there is no policy, bring this issue to the attention of the principal.

If a young person commits suicide, there can be negative repercussions amongst peers, classmates and teachers. It is important not to force students or others into reliving or analyzing the event. Traditional critical incident stress debriefing interventions have not been shown to be helpful and may even cause harm. A supportive space for those students who wish to use it should be provided after school hours and a teacher or guidance counselor known to

Things to look for:
Some young people with ADHD will develop conduct disturbances or substance abuse. Many will become demoralized because of constant reminders from teachers, parents and others about their 'bad behaviour'. Remember that these young people are not bad - they simply have difficulties with sustained attention. Try not to decrease their self-esteem by focusing only on what they have difficulty doing - focus on strengths as well.

the students should ideally be available for those who wish to talk. Each community will have its own traditions for dealing with this kind of event and it is not necessary to create highly effective responses to a suicide in the school setting.

39

What are risk factors for suicide?

The following are the most common (and strongest) risk factors for suicide in young people. Remember that a risk factor does not mean something that causes an event to happen. Rather, it is something that is related to an event that happens.

- Sex (male)
- Depression or other mental disorder
- Previous suicide attempt
- Family history of suicide
- Excessive alcohol or drug use
- Impulsivity or juvenile justice history

Suicide risk is high in people with mental disorders, in particular those with: Depression (of all kinds), Bipolar Disorder (Manic Depression), Schizophrenia, and Substance Abuse. If a young person talks to you about suicide, take them seriously — it is a myth that people who talk about suicide will not attempt suicide.

Questions to ask?

Ask about ideation: "Have you been thinking about dying, harming yourself or suicide?"
Ask about intent: "Have you decided that you would be better off dead or that you should kill yourself?"
Ask about plans: "What plans have you made to kill yourself (and obtain the details)?"

What should I do:

1. If you suspect that a young person may have a mental disorder, it is necessary to refer them to the designated mental health professional (guidance counselor, psychologist, social worker) in the school.
2. If you suspect that a young person may be suicidal, immediately contacting your school designated emergency coordinator or principal is necessary.

PART 3: STUDENT EVALUATION

Student Evaluation

A suggested student evaluation consisting of 28 knowledge questions and 8 attitude questions is available online at: **http://teenmentalhealth.org/curriculum/prepost-student-evaluations/**.

It can also be found from page 43 to 45 of the Guide.

How to Use the Evaluation:

Teachers may wish to use this evaluation before and after teaching the Guide. Teachers who wish to develop their own evaluation methods may do that instead.

Below you'll find the Pre-Curriculum Student Survey for your use.

The correct answers to the Pre-Curriculum Student Survey questions are below the survey, from page 47 to 49 of the Guide.

STUDENT EVALUATION

Pre-*CURRICULUM* STUDENT SURVEY   Date:_____
School Mental Health & *The MENTAL HEALTH & HIGH SCHOOL CURRICULUM GUIDE*

This survey is designed to assess the knowledge regarding school mental health and the Mental Health & High School Curriculum Guide.

What is the name of your school: _____. I identify myself as Male ☐ Female ☐

What Grade are you currently in: 9 ☐   10 ☐ 11 ☐ 12 ☐   Other_____

What English class are you enrolled in at school: Applied ☐   Academic ☐   Other _____

To help us match your anonymous responses between surveys done at the start and end of the course please answer the following questions. These answers allow you to remain anonymous and still allow us to see if your scores on the survey change before and after participating in the class.

a) The name of your first pet _____,

b) Your birth **month** _____, c) Your postal code_____, d) Your shoe size _____,

e) The last two digits/numbers of your home phone number _____.

43

STUDENT EVALUATION

Section A: For each of the following statements select <u>True</u>, <u>False</u>, or <u>Do Not Know</u> by marking an **X** in the appropriate box.

Question	True	False	Do Not Know
1. Mental health and mental illness both involve the brain and how it functions.			
2. People who have mental illness can at the same time have mental health.			
3. The brain can affect the way the body functions but the body can not affect the way the brain functions.			
4. The frontal lobes of a young person's brain continue to grow and develop until about the age of 25 years.			
5. Three of the functions of the brain include thinking, signaling and behavior.			
6. Every person's mood can fluctuate up and down naturally.			
7. The brain acts to help control the functioning of the heart, lungs, and fingers.			
8. Both genetic problems and infections can cause the brain to get sick and stop functioning normally.			
9. The symptoms of mental illness are caused by abnormal functioning of the brain.			
10. People who have a mental illness are frequently violent.			

STUDENT EVALUATION

Question	True	False	Do not know
11. Most people who have a mental illness get well and stay well with treatment.			
12. People who have schizophrenia often get a split personality.			
13. Vitamins and meditation are good treatments for most mental illnesses.			
14. Depression and Bipolar Disorder are two examples of the type of mental illnesses called mood disorders.			
15. An anxiety disorder happens when a person's brain detects the presence of danger – such as a dog attacking.			
16. Panic Disorder commonly begins in adolescence.			
17. A panic attack comes on suddenly and typically lasts one or more days.			
18. Attention Deficit Hyperactivity Disorder has three components including attention problems, hyperactivity, and depression.			
19. Suicide in young people is mostly related to bullying and has little to do with mental illness.			
20. Self-harming behaviors may sometimes accidentally lead to death.			
21. Treatment of mental disorders has three purposes including, relieving symptoms, restoring functioning, and promoting recovery.			
22. People with Social Anxiety Disorder experience irrational and excessive fear that they will act in a way that will be humiliating or embarrassing.			
23. Anorexia Nervosa is an eating disorder that can lead to death.			
24. One important job of the brain is to help the person adapt to the environment.			
25. Mental disorders usually begin because of the stresses of everyday life.			
26. Psychosis is a disturbance in thinking and perception leading to loss of contact with reality.			
27. The main symptoms of Schizophrenia are delusions and hallucinations.			
28. Medicines should be used to treat all mental disorders.			

STUDENT EVALUATION

Section B: This section of the survey is designed to find out about your attitudes toward the statement. For each of the following statements please mark an **X** in the box that you feel best describes your attitude toward the statement. Please select only one answer for each statement.

	Strongly Disagree	Disagree	Disagree a little	Not sure	Agree a little	Agree	Strongly Agree
1. It is easy to tell when someone has a mental illness because they usually act in a strange or bizarre way.							
2. A mentally ill person should not be able to vote in an election.							
3. Most people who have a mental illness are dangerous and violent.							
4. Most people with a mental illness can have a good job and a successful and fulfilling life.							
5. I would be willing to have a person with a mental illness at my school.							
6. I would be happy to have a person with a mental illness become a close friend.							
7. Mental illness is usually a consequence of bad parenting or poor family environment.							
8. People who are mentally ill do not get better.							

SURVEY ANSWER KEY

Section A: For each of the following statements select <u>True</u>, <u>False</u>, or <u>Do Not Know</u> by marking an **X** in the appropriate box.

Question	True	False	Do Not Know
1. Mental health and mental illness both involve the brain and how it functions.	**X**		
2. People who have mental illness can at the same time have mental health.	**X**		
3. The brain can affect the way the body functions but the body can not affect the way the brain functions.		**X**	
4. The frontal lobes of a young person's brain continue to grow and develop until about the age of 25 years.	**X**		
5. Three of the functions of the brain include thinking, signaling and behavior.	**X**		
6. Every person's mood can fluctuate up and down naturally.	**X**		
7. The brain acts to help control the functioning of the heart, lungs, and fingers.	**X**		
8. Both genetic problems and infections can cause the brain to get sick and stop functioning normally.	**X**		
9. The symptoms of mental illness are caused by abnormal functioning of the brain.	**X**		
10. People who have a mental illness are frequently violent.		**X**	

47

SURVEY ANSWER KEY

Question	True	False	Do not know
11. Most people who have a mental illness get well and stay well with treatment.	X		
12. People who have schizophrenia often get a split personality.		X	
13. Vitamins and meditation are good treatments for most mental illnesses.		X	
14. Depression and Bipolar Disorder are two examples of the type of mental illnesses called mood disorders.	X		
15. An anxiety disorder happens when a person's brain detects the presence of danger – such as a dog attacking.		X	
16. Panic Disorder commonly begins in adolescence.	X		
17. A panic attack comes on suddenly and typically lasts one or more days.		X	
18. Attention Deficit Hyperactivity Disorder has three components including attention problems, hyperactivity, and depression.		X	
19. Suicide in young people is mostly related to bullying and has little to do with mental illness.		X	
20. Self-harming behaviors may sometimes accidentally lead to death.	X		
21. Treatment of mental disorders has three purposes including, relieving symptoms, restoring functioning, and promoting recovery.	X		
22. People with Social Anxiety Disorder experience irrational and excessive fear that they will act in a way that will be humiliating or embarrassing.	X		
23. Anorexia Nervosa is an eating disorder that can lead to death.	X		
24. One important job of the brain is to help the person adapt to the environment.	X		
25. Mental disorders usually begin because of the stresses of everyday life.		X	
26. Psychosis is a disturbance in thinking and perception leading to loss of contact with reality.	X		
27. The main symptoms of Schizophrenia are delusions and hallucinations.	X		
28. Medicines should be used to treat all mental disorders.		X	

SURVEY ANSWER KEY

Section B: This section of the survey is designed to find out about your attitudes toward the statement.
For each of the following statements please mark an **X** in the box that you feel best describes your attitude toward the statement. Please select only one answer for each statement.

	Strongly Disagree	Disagree	Disagree a little	Not sure	Agree a little	Agree	Strongly Agree
1. It is easy to tell when someone has a mental illness because they usually act in a strange or bizarre way.	X						
2. A mentally ill person should not be able to vote in an election.	X						
3. Most people who have a mental illness are dangerous and violent.	X						
4. Most people with a mental illness can have a good job and a successful and fulfilling life.							X
5. I would be willing to have a person with a mental illness at my school.							X
6. I would be happy to have a person with a mental illness become a close friend.							X
7. Mental illness is usually a consequence of bad parenting or poor family environment.	X						
8. People who are mentally ill do not get better.	X						

PART 4: MODULES

Module 1:   The Stigma of Mental Illness

Module 2:   Understanding Mental Health and Mental Illness

Module 3:   Information on Specific Mental Illnesses

Module 4:   Experiences of Mental Illness

Module 5:   Seeking Help and Finding Support

Module 6:   The Importance of Positive Mental Health

MODULE 1

The Stigma of Mental Illness

Overview

Many people with mental illness say that the stigma that surrounds mental illness is harder to live with than the disease itself.

Stigma refers to "a cluster of negative attitudes and beliefs that motivate the general public to fear, reject, avoid and discriminate against people with mental illness. Stigma is not just a matter of using the wrong word or action. Stigma is about disrespect. It is the use of negative labels to identify a person living with mental illness. Stigma is a barrier. Fear of stigma and the resulting discrimination discourages individuals and their families from getting the help they need." (SAMHSA, 2004)

In the United States, the Surgeon General's Report on Mental Health (1999) cites studies showing that nearly two-thirds of all people with mental disorders do not seek treatment. While the reasons for this are varied, we know that stigma is a significant barrier that discourages people from seeking treatment.

The activities in this section will explore the nature of stigma, its impact on the lives of people with mental illness, and some ways of combating stigma.

Learning Objectives

In this module students will:

- Understand stigma surrounding mental illness, and the impact of stigma on help-seeking behaviour

- Explore the differences between the myths and realities of mental illness

- Investigate the attitudes of people in the community about mental illness

- Learn about some ways of overcoming stigma and promoting a realistic understanding of mental illness

Major Concepts Addressed

- Stigma results in discriminatory behaviour and treatment towards people with mental illness

- The fear of stigma often prevents people from seeking help and treatment for mental illness

Major Concepts Addressed (cont.)

- Stigma is perpetuated through mistaken beliefs about mental illness, and can be seen in people's attitudes, in public policy, in the media, etc.
- Stigma can be reduced by providing accurate information about mental illness and its treatment

Teacher Background and Preparation

Read through the activities and preview the video component before class. To prepare for Module 1, students need to survey five to ten people about their attitudes toward mental illness.

How-to

Hand out a copy of the Community Attitudes survey and request that students survey a minimum of five and a maximum of ten people from the school, their household or the broader community. Remind students to bring their results in for the lesson.

Activities

- Activity 1: Defining Stigma (10 mins.)
- Activity 2: Exploring Attitudes - Community Survey (10 mins.)
- Activity 3: Video - Digital Story Telling (10 mins.)
- Activity 4: Which Famous People Lived with a Mental Illness? (10 mins.)
- Activity 5: Reducing Stigma - What Works? (10 mins.)
- Activity 6: PowerPoint Presentation: Stigma: Myths and Realities of Mental Illness (10 mins.)

In Advance

- Make photocopies of Activity Handouts one per student
- Support materials

The support materials are located on:
http://teenmentalhealth.org/curriculum/modules/module-1/

The password is: **t33nh3alth**

MODULE 1

Materials Required

- Handouts for Activities 1, 2 and 4
- Videos - Digital Story Telling

Online Supplementary Materials

The supplementary materials are designed to enable you to challenge students in your class to learn more about global issues pertaining to stigma. These may or may not be resources that you wish to employ. Please review them and decide if and how you wish to use them.

Useful Links

Talking about Mental Illness: Teachers' Resource:
http://www.camh.net/education/Resources_teachers_schools/TAMI/tami_teachersresource.html

The World Psychiatric Association program to fight stigma due to Schizophrenia:
http://www.openthedoors.com/

Note to Teachers

Discuss with students the sensitive nature of the questionnaire and warn them that some people they approach might not want to answer it.

Our society often attaches a variety of labels to mental illness - psycho, nuts, crazy, wacko and so on. These terms reinforce the stigma associated with mental illness. In the classroom, it's more appropriate to use the term "person with mental illness".

The following is some general information about Canadian community attitudes towards mental illness and effective ways of addressing mental health problems. You can use this information to compare and contrast with students findings.

According to a 2007 Report on Mental Health Literacy in Canada prepared by the Canadian Alliance on Mental Health and Mental Illness, most Canadians:

- Have difficulty recognizing and correctly identifying mental disorders
- Prefer psychosocial explanations for mental disorders over biomedical ones (e.g. prefer to think that mental illnesses are mostly due to life stress)
- Do not know how to deal with people with mental illnesses
- Associate mental illness with psychotic disorders and are fearful of those labeled "mentally ill"
- Are often reluctant to seek professional help even if they need it
- Have negative attitudes towards medications that effectively treat mental illnesses
- Are often reluctant to disclose mental disorders for fear of stigma and discrimination

Additionally:

- A significant minority of Canadians hold stigmatizing attitudes towards mental illness, and many believe that others subscribe to these views

- Serious mental illness, especially psychosis, is feared and highly stigmatized

- People remain concerned about disclosing their mental illness, particularly in the workplace, for fear of discrimination

MODULE 1

V

Our society often attaches a variety of labels to mental illness which act to reinforce stigma. In the classroom it's more appropriate to use the term "person with mental illness".

Remind students that everyone has some stigmatizing or discriminatory thoughts or attitudes, and that the key message here is that we need to recognize those stigmatizing or discriminatory thoughts or attitudes, examine where they come from, and work toward changing the hurtful behaviours they cause.

Activity 1: (10 mins.)

Defining Stigma

Purpose:

- To explore the meaning of the term stigma and the relationship between attitudes (beliefs) and discriminatory treatment (behaviour and actions) toward people with mental illness.

How-to:

1) Ask students if they know what the word "stigma" means. Lead a whole-class discussion of the definition of stigma, and the relationship between stigma, stereotyping and discrimination.

Questions to Guide Discussion:

- What are some of the negative things you have heard about people with mental illness? Possible answers may include: violence, bizarre behaviour, etc.

- What are some of the positive things you have heard about mental illness? (responses may include: link to creativity). While this may be seen as positive, remind students that generalizing can also be a form of stereotyping.

- Why do you think people with mental illness are stigmatized? (possible answers include: they are seen as being different, people don't really know the facts about mental illness, etc.)

- Can you think of any other health conditions or social issues that have been stigmatized throughout history? (possible answers include: homosexuality, leprosy, AIDS, unwed motherhood, divorce, etc.)

- What kinds of factors have contributed to changing public attitudes around some of these conditions or issues? (possible answers include: education, public policy, open dialogue, scientific research, legislation changing social mores, etc.)

- What do you think influences perceptions about mental illness? (possible answers include: the media – films, news, newspaper headlines and stories that associate people with mental illness with violence, the fact that people with mental illness sometimes behave differently, people are afraid of what they don't understand, etc.)

- How do you think stigma affects the lives of people with mental illness? (possible answers include: people decide not to get help and treatment even though they would benefit from it, it makes them unhappy, they may not be able to get a job or find housing, it may cause them to lose their friends, it puts stress on the whole family, etc.)

*This activity has been adapted from *Talking About Mental Illness*, CAMH 2001
http://www.camh.net/education/Resources_teachers_schools/TAMI/tami_teachersall.pdf

55

MODULE 1

Defining Stigma

The following are definitions of "stigma" taken from different sources and from different historical periods:

> A mark or sign of disgrace or discredit; a visible sign or characteristic of disease.
> - *The Concise Oxford Dictionary, 1990*
>
> An attribute which is deeply discrediting.
> - *Goffman, E. Stigma: The management of Spoiled Identity. 1963*
>
> A distinguishing mark or characteristic of a bad or objectionable kind; a sign of some specific disorder, as hysteria; a mark made upon the skin by burning with a hot iron, as a token of infamy or subjection; a brand; a mark of disgrace or infamy; a sign of severe censure or condemnation, regarded as impressed on a person or thing.
> - *The Shorter Oxford Dictionary, Fourth Edition, 1993*

The Stigma of Mental Illness

"Stigma refers to a cluster of negative attitudes and beliefs that motivate the general public to fear, reject, avoid and discriminate against people with mental illnesses. Stigma is not just a matter of using the wrong word or action. Stigma is about disrespect. It is the use of negative labels to identify a person living with mental illness. Stigma is a barrier. Fear of stigma and the resulting discrimination discourages individuals and their families from getting the help they need." *(SAMHSA 2004)*

Terms Related to Stigma

Stereotype:
"a person or thing that conforms to an unjustly fixed impression or attitude"
Stereotypes are the attitudes about a group of people (e.g. "All people with mental illness are dangerous.")

Prejudice:
"A preconceived opinion"
Prejudice is agreeing with the stereotypes (e.g. "I think people with mental illness are dangerous") without knowing or understanding, literally pre-judging.

Discrimination:
"unfavourable treatment based on prejudice"
Discrimination is a behavior that may result from stigma (e.g. "I don't want people with mental illness around me, therefore I discriminate against them by not hiring them, not being friends with them, etc.")
- *The Concise Oxford Dictionary, 1990*

This activity has been adapted from "Talking About Mental Illness, CAMH 2001

MODULE 1

Activity 2: (10 mins.)

Examining Community Attitudes - Analyzing Survey Results

Purpose:

- To analyze the results of the survey completed by students and discuss in class.
- To compare their results with the Community Attitudes Survey: Best Answers and draw conclusions about the community's awareness of mental health and illness.

How-to:

1) In groups of four or five, students share survey responses to get a better picture of the attitudes of the larger sample. If time permits (or as a possible follow up project for those who are interested), students could use the computer to collate and graph the survey results.

2) Ask students to come up with some general conclusions from the grouped survey findings to share with the rest of the class, for example:

   - Our sample was not well informed about mental illnesses because X% responded…

   - The women in our sample were more tolerant about mental illness than the men

   - Only half the people surveyed agreed that they would have someone with a mental illness as a close friend

3) Facilitate a class-wide discussion about the survey results, highlighting ways in which the results inform us about peoples' attitudes about mental illness. Refer to the Community Attitudes Survey: Best Answers, to ground the discussion and answer any questions that students might have. Use the sample questions below as a guide for discussion.

Sample Questions:

- What do the responses tell you about the level of awareness about mental illness in the community?
- What role do you think the media plays in shaping peoples' attitudes?
- Do you think your results reflect Canada wide community attitudes more generally? Why or why not?
- Do you think it's possible to change community attitudes toward mental illness?
- How might this be done?

MODULE 1

Community Attitudes Survey

Check the most appropriate answer:	Agree	Disagree	Not sure
1) People should work out their own mental health problems			
2) Once you have a mental illness, you have it for life			
3) Females are more likely to have a mental illness than males			
4) Medication is the best treatment for mental illness			
5) People with a mental illness are generally violent and dangerous			
6) Adults are more likely than teenagers to have a mental illness			
7) You can tell by looking at someone whether they have a mental illness			
8) People with a mental illness are generally shy and quiet			
9) Mental illness can happen to anybody			
10) You would be willing to have a person with a mental illness at your school or at your work			
11) You would be happy to have a person with mental illness become a close friend			

Respondent	M/F	Under 19	20-29	30-39	40-49	50 and up
#1						
#2						
#3						
#4						
#5						
#6						
#7						
#8						
#9						
#10						

*Adapted from *MindMatters: Understanding Mental Illness*, pg. 57.

MODULE 1

Community Attitudes Survey: Best Answers

1) People should work out their own mental health problems

Not true. When people have a physical health concern, they generally take some action, and often go to the doctor or seek some other kind of help for their problem. Mental illness is associated with disturbances with brain functioning and usually requires professional assistance. Because of the stigma surrounding mental illness, many people have been reluctant to seek help.

2) Once you have a mental illness, you have it for life

While it's true that most mental illnesses are lifelong, they are often episodic, which means that the symptoms are not always present. Just like people who live with chronic physical illnesses like arthritis and asthma, people with mental illnesses can, when their illness is managed, live positive and productive lives.

3) Females are more likely to have a mental illness than males

Men and women are both equally affected by mental illnesses in general, but there may be higher rates among women of specific illnesses such as eating disorders.
There may sometimes be higher rates in women for other disorders such as depression. Men have higher rates for some disorders such as alcoholism and ADHD. Some illnesses are relatively equally shared by both men and women (e.g. bipolar disorder).

Women are more likely to seek help for mental and emotional difficulties and to share their concerns with friends compared to men. Females are more willing to let friends know if they are receiving counselling. In practice, 62% of women would probably or definitely want their friends to know compared to 45% of men.

Canadian Mental Health Survey COMPAS Inc.
Multi-Audience Research Ottawa and Toronto April 20, 2001)
http://www.cmha.ca/bins/content_page.asp?cid=5-34-212-213#_
Toc512618127

4) Medication is the best treatment for mental illness

Medication can be a very effective part of managing a mental illness, but it is by no means the only type of treatment or support that helps people recover. A wide range of appropriate interventions, including medication, counselling, social, vocational and housing-related supports, as well as self-help and generic resources for all community members (such as: groups, clubs, and religious institutions) are also important in helping people recover and stay well.

It is helpful to think of medications as necessary but not sufficient treatments for many mental disorders. The best approach is to have a combination of strategies that have been proven effective.

5) People with a mental illness are generally violent and dangerous

People with mental illness are generally not more violent than the rest of the population. Mental illness plays no part in the majority of violent crimes committed in our society. The assumption that any and every mental illness carries with it an almost certain potential for violence has been proven wrong in many studies.

6) Adults are more likely than teenagers to have a mental illness

Many of the major mental illnesses begin to appear during adolescence and early adulthood.

7) You can tell by looking at someone whether they have a mental illness

Generally, you can't tell if a person has a mental illness based on their appearance. Sometimes, when people are experiencing an acute episode of their illness, their behaviour may be bizarre, especially if they are experiencing an episode of psychosis.

59

Community Attitudes Survey: Best Answers (cont.)

8) People with a mental illness are generally shy and quiet

There is no strong causal relationship between personality characteristics and tendency to develop mental illness. Some mental disorders such as depression and anxiety can lead people to avoid or limit social contact.

9) Mental illness can happen to anybody

This is correct. In fact, it very likely that you, a family member or someone you're close to will experience a mental illness at some point in their lives.

10) You would be willing to have a person with a mental illness at your school or at your work

11) You would be happy to have a person with mental illness become a close friend

Questions 10 and 11 both address the issue of "social distance" - that is, the willingness to engage in relationships of varying intimacy with a person. Social distance is an indicator of public attitudes toward people with mental illness.

Social distance is a complex concept influenced by a number of factors, including age, gender, socio-economic and cultural factors, but also by the respondent's general attitude toward mental health issues.

Contact, or social inclusion of people with mental illness with the rest of the population, is the factor that usually that leads to a decrease in stigma. This aids in bringing about significant changes in attitudes and behaviour that are maintained over time. This can happen when people find out that a coworker, neighbour or friend is struggling with mental illness, and despite it, is living on their own, working and being a part of the community.

*Adapted from *MindMatters: Understanding Mental Illness*, pg. 57.

MODULE 1

Activity 3: (20 mins.)

Video – Digital Story Telling

Digital Story Telling is the use of a video to tell others about something important in a person's life. In this module, we have placed a number of these digital stories in which youth living with a mental illness have told their story. In addition, we have added a number of made for television advertisements created by young people to point out some issues related to stigma against people living with a mental illness.

Purpose:

- To provide students with an opportunity to learn about the impact of stigma on young people's lives.

- To help students develop an understanding of the living with stigma – the social consequences that are a part of living with a mental illness.

How-to:

1) Set up online video to show the class as a whole or arrange small groups at computers to view Digital Story Telling.

The support materials are located on:
http://teenmentalhealth.org/curriculum/modules/module-1/

The password is: **t33nh3alth**

Please ensure that all students watch at least two different digital stories. Support discussions by asking: what is/are the key message(s); how is the person who is telling the story trying to get their message across; how does what you heard change your ideas about a person living with a mental illness.

MODULE 1

Activity 4: (10 mins.)

Which Famous People Lived with a Mental Illness?

Purpose:

- To help students understand that the presence of a mental illness does not mean a person cannot have a successful life and make a positive contribution to society.

- To demonstrate that people from all walks of life and throughout history have been successful while living with a mental illness.

How-to:

1) Provide students with the following list of names and have them choose (or assign) three to research.

2) Have students complete the following chart for each person named that they will be researching.

3) Have students present their findings to the class.

Name of Person	Area of Greatest Contribution	Type of Mental Illness

List of Names (feel free to add others from your own research): Abraham Lincoln; Winston Churchill; Carrie Fisher; Dorothy Hamill; Clara Hughes; Demi Lovato; Jared Padalecki; Megan Fox; Pete Wentz; David Beckham; Brittany Snow; Josh Ramsay; Beethoven; Leo Tolstoy; Virginia Woolf; Ernest Hemmingway; Margot Kidder; Margaret Trudeau; Ludwig van Patty Duke; Karen Carpenter; Boris Yeltsin; Britney Spears; Charles Darwin; John Nash; Janet Jackson; Buzz Aldrin; Terry Bradshaw; Marlon Brando; Jim Carrey; Robin Williams; Sheryl Crow; Kurt Cobain; Calvin Coolidge; Princess Diana; Tipper Gore; John Daly.

MODULE 1

Activity 5: (10 mins.)

Handout: Reducing Stigma - What Works?

Purpose:

- To provide students with ideas about what they can do to reduce the stigma of mental illness in their everyday lives.

How-to:

1) Distribute the handout (page 65) and encourage students to apply the strategies for reducing stigma in the school, at home, and in the community.

2) Remind students that things have improved since the days of the "looney bin"; however, there are still many examples of how people living with mental illness are portrayed as violent as well as ridiculed in the media and popular culture. Have students think about topical stories from the news and/or movies and TV shows.

MODULE 1

Activity 6: (10 mins.)

PowerPoint Presentation:
Stigma: Myths & Realities of Mental Illness

Purpose:

- To debunk the myths of stigma against mental illness.
- To help understand different types of stigma against mental illness.

How-to:

1) Use the web version of the presentation by logging on to:

http://teenmentalhealth.org/curriculum/wp-content/uploads/2015/06/April2015_
Module-1-PP.compressed-2.pdf

The password is: **t33nh3alth**

Reducing Stigma – What Works?

There is no simple or single strategy to eliminate the stigma associated with mental illness, but some positive steps can be taken. Research is showing that negative perceptions about severe mental illness can be changed by:

- **Providing information based on reliable research** that refutes the mistaken association between violence and severe mental illness.

- **Effective advocacy and public education programs** can help to shift attitudes and contribute to the reduction of stigma.

- **Proximity or direct contact with people with mental illness** tends to reduce negative stereotypes.

- **Programs that help people to become better integrated in the community** through school, work, integrated housing, or interest-based social groups not only serve to promote the individual's mental health by reducing exclusion, but also can play a part in gradually shifting commonly-held negative attitudes.

- **Treatments and supports** that work to help people recover.

MODULE 1

Reducing Stigma – What Works?

LEARN MORE ABOUT MENTAL ILLNESS
If you are well-informed about mental illness, you will be better able to evaluate and resist the inaccurate negative stereotypes that you come across.

LISTEN TO PEOPLE WHO HAVE EXPERIENCED MENTAL ILLNESS
These individuals can describe what they find stigmatizing, how stigma affects their lives and how they would like to be viewed and treated.

WATCH YOUR LANGUAGE
Most of us, even mental health professionals and people who have mental illness, use terms and expressions related to mental illness that may perpetuate stigma.

RESPOND TO STIGMATIZING MATERIAL IN THE MEDIA
Keep your eyes peeled for media that stigmatizes mental illness and report it to any number of organizations. Get in touch with the people - authors, editors, movie producers, advertisers - responsible for the material. Write, call or email them yourself, expressing your concerns and providing more accurate information that they can use.

SPEAK UP ABOUT STIGMA
When someone you know misuses a psychiatric term (such as Schizophrenia), let them know and educate them about the correct meaning. When someone says something negative about a person with mental illness, tells a joke that ridicules mental illness, or makes disrespectful comments about mental illness, let them know that it is hurtful and that you find such comments offensive and unacceptable.

TALK OPENLY ABOUT MENTAL ILLNESS
Don't be afraid to let others know of your mental illness
or the mental illness of a loved one.
The more mental illness remains hidden, the more people continue to believe that it is a shameful thing that needs
to be kept hidden.

DEMAND CHANGE FROM YOUR ELECTED REPRESENTATIVES
Policies that perpetuate stigma can be changed if enough people let their elected representatives, like city councilors, members of Provincial and Federal Parliament know that
they want such change.

PROVIDE SUPPORT FOR ORGANIZATIONS THAT FIGHT STIGMA
Join, volunteer, or donate money. The influence and effectiveness of organizations fighting the stigma surrounding mental illness depend to a large extent on the efforts of volunteers and on donations. You can make a contribution by getting involved.

Adapted from: *Telling is Risky Business: Mental Health Consumers Confront Stigma.* By: Otto Wahl (Rutgers University Press)

MODULE 2

Understanding Mental Health and Mental Illness

Overview

Many young people do not know basic facts about mental health and mental illness. In fact, many people confuse the terms mental health and mental illness. Before thinking about the problems that occur in the brain when someone has a mental illness, it is helpful to think about how the brain functions normally.

In this module, students will be introduced to the basics of brain function, and will learn that the brain processes and reacts to everything we experience. Its activities initiate and control movement, thinking, perception, and involuntary physiological processes (as well as emotions). Students will learn that the brain function determines both mental health and mental illness, and that the two are not mutually exclusive.

Learning Objectives

In this lesson students will learn:

- Some of the basic concepts involved in normal brain function, and the role the brain plays in determining our thoughts, feelings and behaviours

- That mental health and mental illness both include a wide range of states

- That having a mental health problem is not the same thing as having a mental illness

- Some of the language of mental health and mental illness

Major Concepts Addressed

- Everyone has mental health regardless of whether or not they have mental illness.

- The brain is responsible for cognition, perception, emotions, physical functions, signaling (reactions to the environment) and behaviours

- Changes in brain function cause changes in thoughts, feelings and behaviours that can last a short or long time

- A mental illness affects a person's thinking, feelings or behaviour (or all three) and that causes that person difficulty in functioning

- Mental illnesses have complex causes including a biological basis and are therefore not that different from other illnesses

- As with all illnesses, the sooner people get help and treatment for mental illness, the better their long and short-term outcomes

- Many of the major mental illnesses begin to emerge during adolescence

MODULE 2

Understanding Mental Health and Mental Illness (cont.)

Teacher Background

- Read through the activities and definitions provided
- Preview Part 1 of the PowerPoint Presentation:
  Mental Health and Mental Illness : The Common Basis
- Watch the Brain Video: **http://teenmentalhealth.org/curriculum/ modules/module-1/**

Activities

- Activity 1: Language Brainstorm (20 mins.)
- Activity 2: Mental Health and Mental Illness: Language Matters (20 mins.)
- Activity 3: PowerPoint Presentation: Mental Health and Mental Illness: The Common Basis (25 mins.)

In Advance

- Set up computers or projector to show PowerPoint presentation
- Photocopy handouts for Activity 1, one for each student

Materials Required

- Handout Activity 1 Definitions
- Flip chart paper, markers and tape

Online Supplementary Materials

The supplementary materials are designed to challenge students to learn more about the brain. Please review these resources to decide if and how you will use them in your class.

Useful Links

Teen Mental Health (Sun Life Financial Chair in Adolescent Mental Health IWK/Dalhousie University)
http://www.teenmentalhealth.org

MODULE 2

V

It's important to emphasize that there are no wrong answers in a brainstorm. This exercise is all about opening up a discussion. Tell students that they don't have to agree with or believe in the ideas or names they offer.

Activity 1: (20 mins.)

Language Brainstorm

Purpose:

- To provide an icebreaker that encourages students to participate in an open discussion.
- To highlight the ways we tend to conceptualize mental illness as different from physical illness.
- To set the stage for introducing information on mental health and mental illness in the next activity.

How-to:

1) Divide the class into four groups.

2) Give each group a piece of flip chart paper with one of four terms written at the top: Physical health / Mental health / Physical illness / Mental illness.

3) Give the groups five minutes to brainstorm all the words that come to mind when they see their term.

4) After five minutes, ask groups to tape their sheets up on a wall for all groups to see.

5) Ask one student from each group to read out their list for the whole class.

6) Ask students what they notice about the type of words used on each sheet.

7) Discuss the similarities and differences in student responses to mental and physical aspects of people's health.

8) Ask students to suggest some reasons for these differences.

9) Give students handout of definitions of mental health and mental illness and lead a brief discussion on the definitions.

Definitions

Mental Health

There are many different definitions of mental health. They all trying to capture one important thing. That is, that a healthy brain is what gives us mental health. The brain is an important part of the body and the body and brain are linked. It is really not possible to consider them separately. We know that what is good for your body will be good for your brain as well, and vice-versa.

Basically, mental health means having the capacity to be able to successfully adapt to the challenges that life creates for people. These challenges are both positive and negative. In order to adapt to them our brains need to apply all of their capacities of: emotions, cognition/thinking and behaviours. Our brains learn how to apply these capacities over time and as we grow and develop we are able to take on more and more challenges and be successful in dealing with them.

Sometimes people forget that negative emotions are a part of good mental health. Crying, feeling sad occasionally, getting annoyed or angry, etc. are all normal responses to life challenges. So are negative thoughts such as: "this is too hard for me" or "I am not a good person" or "people don't like me". So are negative behaviours, such as yelling at somebody or avoiding a situation that makes us feel stressed. Just because we feel stressed does not mean that we don't have good mental health. Indeed, being able to identify stress and learn how to successfully overcome it in a way that solves the problem causing it is fundamental to having good mental health.

For example: feeling stressed about writing an examination could lead to a negative behaviour – such as going out to party with friends to "forget" about the stress. Or it could lead to a neutral behaviour – such as going for a run or meditating to "release" the stress. But if that is your adaptive response you likely will not do well on your exam. The important coping strategy here is to study or to get help from your teacher to assist you in understanding something that you may not know very well. If you add this coping strategy to your stress "releasing" activity you will be much more likely to succeed and that is a sign of good mental health.

It is important to understand that everyone has mental health just like everyone has physical health. And, just like a person can have good physical health and at the same time have a physical illness, people can have good mental health and a mental illness at the same time.

To understand mental health it is necessary to understand the three related components of mental health: mental distress, mental health problems and mental disorder.

Mental Distress

Mental distress is the inner signal of anxiety or "stress" that a person has when something in their environment is demanding that they adapt to a challenge (for example: writing a test, giving a presentation in front of the class, asking a person to go out on a date, failing to make a school sports team, etc.). This is called a "stress signal" or "stress response". A stress signal has different components to it: emotions/feelings (such as worrying, unhappiness, feeling energized, annoyance), cognitions/thinking (negative thoughts such as "I am no good at anything", "I wish I did not have to do

Definitions (cont.)

this", or positive thoughts such as "this is something I need to solve", "it may be difficult but I can do this", "I should ask my friend for their advice"), physical symptoms (such as stomach aches and headaches, the stomach "butterflies") and behaviours (such as avoidance of the situation, engagement of the challenge, positive energy, withdrawal from others, yelling at someone or helping someone). As we can see, the response to distress can have both negative and positive components! We need to make sure we don't always focus on the negative ones.

Everybody experiences mental distress (often called "stress") everyday. It is a part of good mental health. It is a signal that tells us to try something new to solve the challenge we are facing. As the person who feels distress tries to develop solutions or strategies to solve the challenges (often called "stressors") they figure out what works and what does not work well. Successfully dealing with the stressor (also called solving the problem) leads to learning what strategy worked and use of that strategy in similar situations in the future. Once the person has successfully overcome the challenge, the distress goes away. But the learning and skill sets remain, ready to be used another time.

Young people experiencing everyday mental distress do not require counselling, they are not "sick" and they do not need treatment. They can learn how to manage stress and how to use the "stress signal" to learn new skills. They learn these skills by trial and error, by obtaining advice from friends, parents, teachers and trusted adults and from other sources (such as the media). They can also use techniques that are part of general health management, such as: exercise, having enough sleep, being with friends and family, eating properly and staying away from drugs and alcohol. Sometimes what the young person tries

does not work (for example: instead of studying for an exam they go out and party with their friends, instead of getting a good night's sleep before an exam they try to stay up all night and study) and as a result their distress may increase. But making wrong choices is part of learning how to make good choices. This is a normal part of growing up. Allowing young people to avoid everyday mental distress can have negative impacts on their development of skills that they need to learn in order to have successful adult lives.

Mental Health Problems

Mental health problems arise when a person is faced with a much larger stressor than usual. For example: death of a loved one, moving to a new country, having a serious physical illness, etc. When faced with these large stressors, everyone experiences strong negative emotions (such as: sadness, grief, anger, demoralization, etc.). These emotions are also accompanied by substantial difficulties in other domains such as: cognitive/thinking (for example: "nothing will ever be the same", "I don't know if I can go on in my life", etc.), physical (for example: sleep problems, loss of energy, numerous aches and pains), and behavioural (for example: social withdrawal, avoidance of usual activities, angry outbursts, etc.).

Sometimes the young person experiencing a mental health problem will exhibit noticeable difficulties in everyday functioning - at school and outside of school. In addition to the distress management skills and general health enhancing activities that are useful in decreasing mental distress, young people experiencing a mental health problem will often need additional support to help them through the difficult situation or assist them with problems in functioning (such as extra time for academic activities, time away from school to be with their families, etc.). In such cases, this support can come from a counselor, a religious leader, or another person that has the skills needed to help effectively. Medical treatment is usually not necessary.

Definitions (cont.)

Mental Illness

A mental illness is very different from mental distress and from a mental health problem. It arises from a complex interplay between a person's genetic makeup and the environment in which they live. A mental illness (also called a mental disorder) is a medical condition diagnosed by trained health professionals (such as doctors, mental health clinicians, psychiatric nurses and psychologists) using internationally established diagnostic criteria. A person with a mental disorder is best helped by a trained health professional providing best evidence-based treatments. Mental illnesses are the result of changes that arise in usual brain function as a result of a complex interplay between a person's genes and environment. When a person has a mental disorder, their brain is not working as it should be.

A person with a mental illness will experience significant, substantial and persistent challenges with emotions/feelings (for example: depression, panic attacks, overwhelming anxiety, etc.), cognition/thinking (delusions, disordered thoughts, hopelessness, suicidal thoughts, etc.), physical (for example: fatigue, lethargy, excessive movement, etc.), and behavioural (for example: school refusal and withdrawal from family and friends, suicide attempt, poor self-care, etc.). The presence of a mental disorder signifies that an individual needs best evidence-based interventions of many different types (such as medications, psychotherapies, social interventions, etc.), provided by appropriately trained health providers. While interventions that can help distress and mental health problems can also be used to help a person who has a mental illness, and general health enhancing activities are always useful, a young person with a mental disorder requires a degree of care above and beyond that usually provided for a mental health problem. Mental disorders always require treatment using best evidence-based care by trained health professionals (such as: mental health officers, doctors, psychiatric nurses, psychologists, etc.).

And: a person can be in each of these states at the same time. For example, over the course of one day a person can be laughing and having fun with their friends (no distress, problem or disorder), can experience distress (lost his/her house key), be experiencing a mental health problem (their uncle with whom they were close died earlier this week), and have a mental disorder (such as Attention Deficit Hyperactivity Disorder).

Glossary

In Module 2 there is a mental health glossary. Consider making some copies for the class or send students to **www.teenmentalhealth.org** to find it.

MODULE 2

Activity 2: (20 mins.)

Mental Health and Mental Illness: Language Matters

Purpose:

- To help understand how the words that we use can help us better understand what mental health state category others or we are in.
- To learn how to use specific words to more clearly describe how we are feeling.

How-to:

1) Provide the class with the following list of words, which all describe emotional states.

2) Prepare four sections along the wall of the classroom (or four different flip charts) with each titled as one of the four different mental health states.

3) Have each student write each word on a sticky note corresponding to the mental health state category that they think best captures the meaning of the word.

4) Once they are finished, have students place their words in the mental health state categories as you have prepared them.

5) Discuss which words are most commonly used for each category and why some words may be less appropriate for certain categories.

Word list: upset, annoyed, sad, unhappy, disappointed, disgusted, demoralized, angry, disappointed, bitter, blue, heartbroken, down, sorry, sorrowful, glum, forlorn, pensive, thoughtful, disconsolate, distressed, despondent, depressed, dejected, pessimistic, mournful, despairing, Depression.

Note: here the word "Depression" would be used to denote the mental illness of Depression while the word "depressed" would be used to denote a negative emotional state which may better fit in the category of mental health problem.

What does it Mean?

If students do not know the meaning of a word, they need to find out as part of this activity.

73

MODULE 2

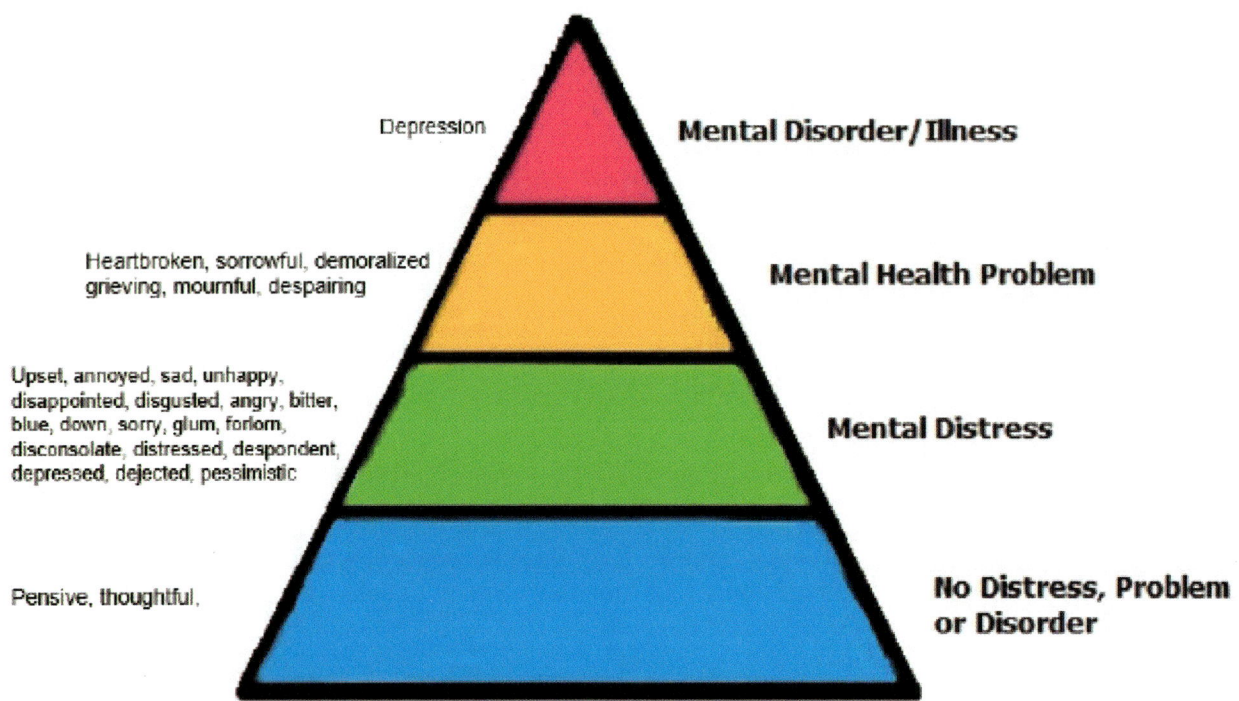

The inter-relationship of mental health states

Depression — **Mental Disorder/Illness**

Heartbroken, sorrowful, demoralized grieving, mournful, despairing — **Mental Health Problem**

Upset, annoyed, sad, unhappy, disappointed, disgusted, angry, bitter, blue, down, sorry, glum, forlorn, disconsolate, distressed, despondent, depressed, dejected, pessimistic — **Mental Distress**

Pensive, thoughtful. — **No Distress, Problem or Disorder**

Note to Teachers:

- Mental health states are not a continuum. People do not usually progress from mental distress to illness.

- People can experience one or more states at the same time.

- Different mental health states should be dealt with differently. For example, daily mental distress may not need any intervention. People are able to adapt by themselves with support from the family or community. People with mental health problems may need extra professional help, such as counseling, in addition to family and community support. People with mental disorders require best evidence-based care from properly trained health care providers.

Glossary

In Module 2 there is a mental health glossary. Consider making some copies for the class or send students to **www.teenmentalhealth.org** to find it.

MODULE 2

Activity 3: (25 mins.)

PowerPoint Presentation:
Mental Health and Mental Illness: The Common Basis

Purpose:

- To provide an introduction to basic brain functioning for students to help them understand that the brain controls cognition, perception, emotions, physical functions, signaling (reactions to the environment) and behaviours.

- To illustrate that mental health and mental illness are related to each other, and that they are not mutually exclusive.

- To show that some changes in brain function cause changes in thoughts, feelings and behaviour that last a short or a long time.

How-to:

1) Use the web version of the presentation by logging on to:

http://teenmentalhealth.org/curriculum/wp-content/uploads/2014/07/Module_2_-_2013.pdf

The password is: **t33nh3alth**

See Module 2/Activity 2: Mental Health and Mental Illness: The Common Basis.

MODULE 3

Information on Specific Mental Illnesses

Overview

In this module, students will learn more about the most common mental illnesses that affect adolescents.

Learning Objectives

In this module, students will:

- Recognize that mental illnesses are associated with differences in brain functions
- Gain a better understanding of the symptoms, causes, treatments and other supports for specific mental illnesses that are common among adolescents

Major Concepts Addressed

- A mental illness changes many aspects of a person's life (cognition, perception, emotions, physical functions, signaling (reactions to the environment and behaviours) and causes that person difficulty in functioning
- Mental illness describes a broad range of conditions. The type, intensity, and duration of symptoms of mental illnesses vary
- The exact cause of mental disorders is not known, but most experts believe that a combination of biological and environmental factors are involved
- Like illnesses that affect other parts of the body, mental illnesses are treatable, and the sooner people receive proper treatment and supports, the better the outcomes
- With a variety of supports, most people with mental illness recover and go on to lead fulfilling and productive lives

Teacher Background and Preparation

- Read through the information sheets for Activity 2 on mental illnesses prior to the class
- Preview the PowerPoint presentation
- Review Teacher Knowledge Update

MODULE 3

Activities

Activity 1:   PowerPoint Presentation:
                What Happens When the Brain Gets Sick? (10 mins.)
Activity 2:   PowerPoint Presentation:
                Common Mental Illnesses (20 mins.)
Activity 3:   Specialist groups – Learning about Specific Mental
                Illnesses (20 mins.)
Activity 4:   Sharing the pieces (10 mins)

In Advance

- Preview both PowerPoint presentations

- Preview each of the seven animated videos

- Photocopy Activity 3 handouts and information sheets on specific mental illnesses (there are eight illnesses covered)

- We also recommend teachers print the "TMH Speaks ... Mags" Series from **www.teenmentalhealth.org/toolbox** and distribute to students for use in the classroom

Materials Required

- PowerPoint presentations
- Handouts: Activity 3 Activity sheets

Online Supplementary Materials

The supplementary materials are designed to enable you to challenge students in your class to learn more about different mental disorders. These may or may not be resources you wish to employ. Please review them and decide if and how you wish to use them. We suggest using the online "TMH Speaks ... Mini Mags" Series as a resource for Activity 3. The resource can be found in the "Useful Links" section below.

If you are also using Teacher Knowledge Update, print as many copies as you think will be necessary for your class.

Useful Links

Sun Life Financial Chair in Adolescent Mental Health:
 "TMH Speaks ... Mini Mags" Series: http://www.teenmentalhealth.org/toolbox

Mood Disorders
Mood Magazine: http://www.moodsmag.com/

Useful Links (cont.)

Mood Disorders Association of Ontario (MDAO):
http://www.mooddisorders.ca/

Schizophrenia:
Schizophrenia Society of Canada:
http://www.schizophrenia.ca/

Anxiety disorder:
Anxiety Disorders Association of Canada:
http://www.anxietycanada.ca/

Obsessive-Compulsive Foundation:
http://www.ocfoundation.org/

Anxiety Disorders Association of America:
http://www.adaa.org/

Eating Disorder:
National Eating Disorder Information Centre:
http://www.nedic.ca

Bulimia Anorexia Nervosa Association:
http://www.bana.ca

MODULE 3

Activities 1 & 2: (30 mins.)

PowerPoint Presentations:
What Happens When the Brain Gets Sick? and Common Mental Illnesses

Purpose:

- The PowerPoint "What Happens When the Brain Gets Sick?" provides an overview of how the six different brain functions change between a healthy brain and when a mental illness occurs.

- Students should understand that a mental disorder is due to changes in usual brain function.

- The PowerPoint "Common Mental Illnesses" provides an overview of the common mental illnesses.

- Students should conduct further study into the various mental illnesses as outlined in activities 3 and 4.

How-to:

1) Use the PowerPoint "What Happens When the Brain Gets Sick?" from the web:

   http://teenmentalhealth.org/curriculum/wp-content/uploads/2014/08/Module_3_
   Part_1_2014.pdf

   The password is: **t33nh3alth**

2) Use the PowerPoint "Common Mental Illnesses" from the web:

   http://teenmentalhealth.org/curriculum/wp-content/uploads/2014/08/Module_3_
   Part_2_2014.pdf

   The password is: **t33nh3alth**

MODULE 3

Activity 3: (20 mins.)

Discussion Groups

Purpose:

- To provide information about various common mental disorders.
- To have students learn about these disorders and share their learning with others.

How-to:

1) Explain to students that a jigsaw puzzle activity will be used during this lesson. This means that students will work in small groups and will become resource persons about one mental illness (one piece of the jigsaw). After completing the handout on their specific illness together, they will break up into mixed groups to share their information and learn more about the other illnesses from the other members of the group.

2) Give the groups a few minutes to scan the information sheets and direct them to the online "TMH Speaks ... Mini Mags" Series at **http://www.teenmentalhealth.org/toolbox**. When they have finished reviewing, ask each group to discuss the mental illness they were assigned.

3) Have each group complete the handouts to share with others during the next activity.

Group 1: Anxiety Disorders

What is Anxiety?

Anxiety is a term which describes a normal feeling people experience when faced with threat or danger, or when stressed. Indeed, anxiety (commonly called stress) often has a useful adaptive function. It is a signal that we need to do something to adapt to a change in our environment. It is part of the signaling function of the brain. This normal kind of anxiety is always caused by an environmental change (for example: a test, going on a date, speaking out in class, playing an important game, etc.).

When people become anxious they typically feel upset, uncomfortable and tense and may experience many physical symptoms such as stomach upset, shaking and headaches.

Feelings of anxiety are caused by experiences of life such as a new relationship, a new job or school, illness or an accident. Feeling anxious is appropriate in these situations and usually we feel anxious for only a limited time. These feelings are not regarded as an illness, but are a part of everyday life.

What are Anxiety Disorders?

The Anxiety Disorders are a group of illnesses, each characterized by persistent feelings of intense anxiety. There are feelings of continual or extreme discomfort and tension, and may include panic attacks. This anxiety also comes by itself, not as part of a change in the person's environment.

People are likely to be diagnosed with an Anxiety Disorder when their level of anxiety or feelings of panic are so extreme that they significantly interfere with daily life and stop them from doing what they want to do. This is what characterizes an Anxiety Disorder as more than normal feelings of anxiety.

Anxiety Disorders affect the way the person thinks, feels and behaves and, if not treated, cause considerable suffering and life difficulties. They often begin in adolescence or early adulthood and may sometimes be triggered by significant stress. People with an Anxiety Disorder also usually show much more anxiety when faced with an everyday environmental challenge compared to a person without an Anxiety Disorder.

Anxiety Disorders are common and may affect one in twenty people at any given time.

Anxiety Disorders: What are the Main Types of Anxiety Disorders?

All Anxiety Disorders are disturbances of the brain's signaling functions and are characterized by heightened anxiety or panic as well as significant problems in everyday life.

Generalized Anxiety Disorder

People with this disorder worry constantly about themselves or their loved ones, financial disaster, their health, work or personal relationships. These people experience continual apprehension and often suffer from many physical symptoms such as headache, diarrhea, stomach pains and heart palpitations.

Agoraphobia

Agoraphobia is fear of being in places or situations from which it may be difficult or embarrassing to get away, or a fear that help might be unavailable in the event of having a panic attack.

People with agoraphobia most commonly experience fear in a cluster of situations: in supermarkets and department stores, crowded places of all kinds, confined spaces, public transport, elevators, highways, etc.

People experiencing agoraphobia may find comfort in the company of a safe person or object. This may be a spouse, friend, pet or medicine carried with them.

The onset of agoraphobia is common between the ages of 15 and 20, and is often associated with Panic Disorder or Social Anxiety Disorder.

Panic Disorder (With or Without Agoraphobia)

People with this disorder experience panic attacks in situations where most people would not be afraid such as: at home, walking in the park or going to a movie. These attacks occur spontaneously, come on rapidly (over a few minutes) and go away slowly. Usually they last about 10-15 minutes.

The attacks are accompanied by all of the unpleasant physical symptoms of anxiety, with a fear that the attack may lead to a total loss of control or death.

It is because of this that some people start to experience a fear of going to places where panic attacks may occur and of being in places where help is not at hand. In addition to panic attacks and agoraphobia symptoms, people with panic disorder also worry about having another panic attack.

Specific Phobias

Everyone has some mild irrational fears, but phobias are intense fears about particular objects or situations which interfere with our lives or harm us. These might include fear of heights, water, dogs, closed spaces snakes or spiders.

Someone with a specific phobia is fine when the feared object is not present. However, when faced with the feared object or situation, the person can become highly anxious and experience a panic attack.

People affected by phobias can go to great lengths to avoid situations which would force them to confront the object or situation which they fear.

Social Anxiety Disorder

People with Social Anxiety Disorder fear that others will judge everything they do in a negative way and they feel easily embarrassed in most social situations. They believe they may be considered to be flawed or worthless if any sign of poor performance is detected.

They cope by either trying to do everything perfectly, limiting what they are doing in front of others (especially eating, drinking, speaking or writing) or withdrawing gradually from contact with others. They will often experience panic symptoms in social situations and will avoid many situations where they feel observed by others (such as: in stores, movie theatres, public speaking and social events).

Anxiety Disorders: What are the Main Types of Anxiety Disorders? (cont.)

Anxiety Disorders are among the most common of the mental illnesses. About 5-8% of people can be expected to experience an Anxiety Disorder during their adolescent years.

For more information on some Anxiety Disorders, check out:

http://issuu.com/weusthem/docs/magazine_ panic/1?e=8480834/6664696

http://issuu.com/weusthem/docs/magazine_ social_anxiety/1?e=8480834/6664692

What Causes Anxiety Disorders?

The causes of each disorder may vary, and it is not always easy to determine the causes in every case. All Anxiety Disorders are associated with abnormalities in the brain signaling mechanisms that are involved in the creation and expression of "normal" anxiety.

Personality

People with certain personality characteristics may be more prone to Anxiety Disorders. Those who are easily upset are very sensitive, emotional or avoidant of others may be more likely to develop Anxiety Disorders.

Learned Response

Some people exposed to situations, people or objects that are upsetting or anxiety-producing may develop an anxiety response when faced with the same situation, person or object again, or become anxious when thinking about the situation, person or object. This is not likely to lead to an Anxiety Disorder.

Heredity

The tendency to develop Anxiety Disorders has a genetic basis and runs in families.

Biochemical Processes

All Anxiety Disorders arise from disturbances in the different brain areas or connections amongst the areas that comprise the signaling circuitry of the brain.

How Can Anxiety Disorders be Treated?

If they are not effectively treated, Anxiety Disorders may interfere significantly with a person's thinking and behaviour. This can cause considerable suffering and distress. Some Anxiety Disorders may precede Depression or Substance Abuse and in such cases treatment may help to prevent these problems.

Many professionals such as family doctors, psychologists, social workers, counselors or psychiatrists can help people deal with Anxiety Disorders.

Treatment will often include education and specific types of psychotherapy (such as cognitive behavioural therapy) to help the person understand their thoughts, emotions and behaviour. People develop new ways of thinking about their anxiety and how to deal more effectively with feelings of anxiety.

Medication is sometimes used to help the person control their high anxiety levels, panic attacks or Depression.

The Benzodiazepines (such as diazepam) are used for the temporary relief of anxiety, but care has to be taken as these medications may occasionally cause difficulties in some people.

Antidepressants play an important role in the treatment of some Anxiety Disorders, as well as associated or underlying depression. Contrary to common belief, antidepressants are not addictive.

MODULE 3

Group 1: Understanding Anxiety Disorders

What are Anxiety Disorders?

How common are Anxiety Disorders?

Describe some of the symptoms of Anxiety Disorders:

List and briefly explain some of the main types of Anxiety Disorders:

What type of treatment is available for people experiencing Anxiety Disorders?

What other kinds of support can help people with Anxiety Disorders recover?

Group 2: Attention Deficit Hyperactivity Disorder (ADHD)

What is Attention Deficit Hyperactivity Disorder (ADHD)?

Attention Deficit Hyperactivity Disorder is the most commonly diagnosed behavioural disorder of childhood.

ADHD affects an estimated 4 -6 % of young people between the ages of 9 and 20. Boys are two to three times more likely than girls to develop ADHD. Although ADHD is usually associated with children, the disorder can persist into adulthood. Children and adults with ADHD are easily distracted by sights, sounds, and other features of their environment. They cannot concentrate for long periods of time, are restless and impulsive, or have a tendency to daydream and be slow to complete tasks.

Symptoms

The three predominant symptoms of ADHD are 1) inability to regulate activity level (hyperactivity), 2) inability to attend to tasks (inattention), and 3) impulsivity, or inability to inhibit behaviour.

Common symptoms include varying degrees of the following:

- Poor concentration and brief attention span
- Increased activity - always on the go
- Impulsive - does not stop to think
- Social and relationship problems
- Fearless and takes undue risks
- Poor coordination
- Sleep problems
- Normal or high intelligence but under-performing at school

All must occur with greater frequency and intensity than "normal" and must lead to functional impairment as a result of the symptoms in order to be considered ADHD.

What Causes ADHD?

While no one really knows what causes ADHD, it is generally agreed by the medical and scientific community that ADHD is due to problems in the brain's control of systems that regulate concentration, motivation and attention.

Much of today's research suggests that genetics play a major role in ADHD. The possibility of a genetic cause to ADHD is supported by the fact that ADHD runs in families. About 70% of children with ADHD have a first-degree relative with ADHD. Approximately half of parents who have been diagnosed with ADHD themselves will have a child with the disorder.

It has been generally considered that approximately 70% of ADHD cases can be explained by genetics. It is obvious that not every case of ADHD can be explained by genetics; there are other causes of ADHD.

Researchers have suggested that some of the following could also be responsible for ADHD symptoms:

- exposure to toxins (such as lead)
- injuries to the brain
- a traumatic birth process

However, all of these possibilities need further research.

Many people with ADHD will also have a specific learning difficulty, such as problems with spelling, mathematics, etc. Some studies suggest that about 30% of adolescents with ADHD may have a learning difficulty.

Attention Deficit Hyperactivity Disorder (ADHD)

Myths, Misunderstandings and Facts

According to the National Institutes of Mental Health, ADHD is not caused by:

- Too much TV
- Sugar
- Caffeine
- Food colourings
- Poor home life
- Poor schools
- Food allergies

How can ADHD be treated?

A variety of medications and behavioural interventions are used to treat ADHD. The most effective treatments are medications. The most widely used medications are stimulants such as methylphenidate. Nine out of ten children improve when taking one of these medications. These medications are safe when used as prescribed by qualified physicians. Some common side effects are decreased appetite and insomnia. These side effects generally occur early in treatment and often decrease over time. Some studies have shown that the stimulants used to treat ADHD slow growth rate, but ultimate height is not affected.

Interventions used to help treat ADHD include several forms of psychotherapy such as cognitive-behavioural therapy, social skills training, support groups, and parent and educator skills training. A combination of medication and psychotherapy may be more effective than medication treatment alone in improving social skills, parent-child relations, reading achievement and aggressive symptoms.

For more information on ADHD, check out:

**http://issuu.com/weusthem/docs/magazine_
adhd/3?e=8480834/6664699**

MODULE 3

Group 2: Understanding Attention Deficit Hyperactivity Disorder (ADHD)

What is ADHD?

How common is ADHD?

Describe some of the symptoms of ADHD:

What type of treatment is available for people experiencing ADHD?

What other kinds of support can help people with ADHD recover?

Group 3: Bipolar Mood Disorder

Bipolar Mood Disorder is the new name for what was once called manic depressive illness. The new name is used as it better describes the extreme mood swings - from depression and sadness to elation and excitement – that people with this illness experience.

People with Bipolar Mood Disorder experience recurrent episodes of depressed and elated moods. Both can be mild to severe.

What are the symptoms of Bipolar Mood Disorder?

Mania - Common symptoms include varying degrees of the following:

- **Elevated mood** – The person feels extremely high, happy and full of energy. The experience is often described as feeling on top of the world and being invincible.

- **Increased energy and over-activity**

- **Reduced need for sleep**

- **Irritability** – The person may easily and frequently get angry and irritable with people who disagree or dismiss their sometimes unrealistic plans or ideas.

- **Rapid thinking and speech** – Thoughts are more rapid than usual. This can lead to the person speaking quickly and jumping from subject to subject.

- **Lack of inhibitions** – This can be the result of the person's reduced ability to foresee the consequences of their actions. For example, spending large amounts of money buying things they don't really need.

- **Grandiose plans and beliefs** – It is common for people experiencing mania to believe that they are unusually talented or gifted or are kings, movie stars or political leaders. It is common for religious beliefs to intensify or for people with this illness to believe they are an important religious figure.

- **Lack of insight** – A person experiencing mania may understand that other people see their ideas and actions as inappropriate, reckless or irrational. However, they are unlikely to recognize the behaviour as inappropriate in themselves.

- **Psychosis** – Some people with mania or depression experience psychotic symptoms such as hallucinations and delusions.

Depression

- **Lowered mood** – Many people with Bipolar Mood Disorder experience depressive episodes. This type of Depression can be triggered by a stressful event, but more commonly occurs without obvious cause.

- **Withdrawal** – The person loses interest and pleasure in activities they previously enjoyed. They may withdraw and stop seeing friends, avoid social activities and cease simple tasks such as shopping and showering.

- **Loss of appetite or weight** – They may become overwhelmed by Depression, lose their appetite, lose weight, become unable to concentrate, and may experience feelings of guilt or hopelessness.

- **Feelings of hopelessness** – Some attempt suicide because they believe life has become meaningless or they feel too guilty to go on.

- **Delusions** – Others develop false beliefs (delusions) of persecution or guilt, or think that they are evil.

- For more information on Depression and its treatment, please see the information sheet called "What is Depression?"

MODULE 3

Bipolar Mood Disorder (cont.)

Normal Moods

Most people who have episodes of Mania and Depression experience normal moods in between. They are able to live productive lives, manage household and business commitments and hold down a job.

Everyone experiences mood swings from time-to-time. It is when these moods become extreme and lead to a failure to cope with life that medical attention is necessary.

What Causes Bipolar Mood Disorder?

Bipolar Mood Disorder affects one to two people in every hundred in the Canadian population. Men and women have an equal chance of developing the disorder. It usually appears when people are in their twenties, but often begins in the teen years.

It is believed that Bipolar Mood Disorder is caused by a combination of factors including genetics.

Genetic Factors

Studies on close relations, identical twins and adopted children whose natural parents have Bipolar Mood Disorder strongly suggest that the illness may be genetically transmitted, and that children of parents with Bipolar Mood Disorder have a greater risk of developing the disorder.

Biochemical Factors

Mania, like Major Depression, is believed to be associated with chemical changes or other problems in how nerves in the brain communicate which can often be corrected with medication.

Stress

Stress may play a role in triggering symptoms, but not usually. Often the illness itself may cause the stressful event (such as divorce or a failed business), which may then be blamed for causing the illness. Drugs or other physical stressors (such as jet lag) may bring on an episode.

Seasons

Mania is more common in the spring, and Depression in the early winter. The reason for this is not clear, but it is thought to be associated with the light/dark cycle, and the amount of total daily sunshine.

How Can Bipolar Disorder be Treated?

- Effective treatments are available for depressive and manic episodes of Bipolar Mood Disorder. Medications called thymoleptics (such as lithium) are an essential treatment for the entire course of the illness.

- Antidepressant medications are effective for the depressive phase of the illness. Bright light therapy and some psychological treatments may also help.

- Antidepressants are not addictive. They slowly return the balance of neurotransmitters in the brain, taking four to six weeks to achieve their positive effects.

- Medication should be adjusted only under medical supervision as some people may experience a switch to a manic phase if given an antidepressant.

- Several different medications may be used during acute or severe attacks of mania. Some are specifically used to calm the person's manic excitement; others are used to help stabilize the person's mood. Medications such as lithium are also used as preventive measures as they help to control mood swings and reduce the frequency and severity of both depressive and manic phases.

- It may be necessary to admit a person with severe Depression or Mania to a hospital for some time.

- It can often be difficult to persuade someone that they need treatment when they are in a manic phase.

- Psychotherapy and counseling are used with medication to help the person understand the illness and better manage its effects on their life.

- With access to appropriate treatment and support, most people with Bipolar Mood Disorder lead full and productive lives.

For more information on Bipolar Disorder, check out:

http://issuu.com/weusthem/docs/magazine_bipolar/1?e=8480834/6664704

Group 3: Understanding Bipolar Mood Disorder

What is Bipolar Mood Disorder?

How common is Bipolar Mood Disorder?

Describe some of the symptoms of Bipolar Mood Disorder:

What combination of factors is believed to cause Bipolar Mood Disorder?

What type of treatment is available for people experiencing Bipolar Mood Disorder?

What other kinds of support can help a person with Bipolar Mood Disorder recover?

Group 4: Depression

What is Depression?

The word Depression is often used to describe the feelings of sadness which all of us experience at some point in our lives. It is also a term used to describe a form of mental illness called Clinical Depression or just Depression.

Because Depression is so common, it is important to understand the difference between unhappiness or sadness in daily life and the symptoms of clinical depression.

When faced with stress (such as the loss of a loved one, relationship breakdown or great disappointment or frustration), most people will feel unhappy or sad. These are emotional reactions which are appropriate to the situation and will usually last only a limited time. These reactions are not a Depression, but are a part of everyday life.

The term Depression describes not just one illness, but a group of illnesses characterized by excessive or long-term depressed mood which affects the person's life. Depression is often accompanied by feelings of anxiety. Whatever the symptoms and causes of Depression, there are many therapeutic interventions which are effective.

To help differentiate the symptom of "depression" from the mental disorder "Depression" we capitalize the "D" in the illness.

What are the Main Types of Depressive Illness?

Adjustment Disorders with depressed mood

People with this problem are reacting to distressing situations in their lives (e.g., the failure of a close relationship or loss of a job) but to a greater degree than usual.

This Depression is more intense than the unhappiness experienced in daily life. It lasts longer and the symptoms often include anxiety, poor sleep and a loss of appetite. This form of Depression may last longer than a few weeks.

It usually goes away when the cause is removed or the person finds a new way to cope with the stress. Occasionally people require professional help to overcome this type of Depression.

"Baby Blues" and Postpartum Depression

The so-called "baby blues" affect about half of all new mothers. They feel mildly depressed, anxious, tense or unwell, and may have difficulty sleeping even though they are tired and lethargic most of the time. These feelings may last only hours or a few days, then disappear. Professional help is not usually needed. This is not Depression.

However, in up to ten percent of mothers this feeling of sadness develops into a serious disorder called Postpartum Depression. Mothers with this illness find it increasingly difficult to cope with the demands of everyday life.

They can experience anxiety, fear, despondency and sadness. Some mothers may have panic attacks or become tense and irritable. There may be a change in appetite and sleep patterns. Because of these symptoms they may have difficulties in their daily lives, including trouble in caring for their child.

A severe, but rare form of Postpartum Depression is called Puerperal Psychosis. The woman is unable to cope with her everyday life and is disturbed in her thinking and behaviour. Professional help is needed for both Postpartum Depression and Puerperal Psychosis.

Major Depressive Disorder

This is the most common form of Depression. It can come on without apparent cause, although in some cases a severely distressing event might trigger the condition.

The cause is not well understood but is believed to be associated with a chemical or other problem in the parts of the brain that control mood. Genetic predisposition is common.

Depression (cont.)

A Depression can develop in people who have coped well with life, who are good at their work, and who are happy in family and social relationships.

For no apparent reason, they can become low-spirited, lose their enjoyment of life and suffer from disturbed sleep patterns. People experiencing Depression have severe emotional thinking, behavioural and physical symptoms.

Sometimes feelings of hopelessness and despair can lead to thoughts of suicide. Suicide is a tragic outcome of Depression in some people.

The most serious form of this type of Depression is called Psychotic Depression. During this illness, the person loses touch with reality, may stop eating and drinking and may hear voices saying they are wicked, or worthless or deserve to be punished.

Others develop false beliefs (delusions) that they have committed bad deeds in the past and deserve to be punished, or falsely believe that they have a terminal illness such as cancer (despite there being no medical evidence).

A Depression is a serious illness which present risks to the person's life and well-being. Professional assessment and treatment is always necessary and, in severe cases, hospitalization may be required.

Bipolar Mood Disorder

A person with Bipolar Mood Disorder experiences Depression with periods of Mania which involve extreme happiness, over-activity, rapid speech, a lack of inhibition and in more serious instances, psychotic symptoms including hearing voices and delusions of grandeur.

Sometimes only periods of Mania occur without depressive episodes, but this is rare. More information about this mood disorder is found in the section called "What is Bipolar Mood Disorder?"

What Causes Depression?

Depression is caused by a combination of environmental and genetic factors. Depression "runs" in families but most people who have a family member with Depression do not develop the illness.

Depression may also be associated with stress after personal tragedies or disasters. It is more common at certain stages of life (such as at childbirth). It may also occur with some physical illnesses. However, Depression often causes life stresses which are incorrectly considered to be causes of Depression.

Depression (cont.)

How Can Depression be Treated?

People experiencing Depression should contact their family doctor or community health centre. Treatments for Depression can help the person return to more normal feelings and to enjoy life. The approach depends on each person's symptoms and circumstances, but will generally take one or more of the following forms:

- Psychological interventions help individuals understand their thoughts, behaviours and interpersonal relationships.

- Antidepressant medications relieve depressed feelings, restore normal sleep patterns and appetite, and reduce anxiety. Antidepressant medications are not addictive. They slowly return the balance of neurotransmitters in the brain, taking four to six weeks to achieve their positive effects.

- Specific medications help to manage mood swings for people with Bipolar Illness.

- General supportive counseling assists people in sorting out practical problems and conflicts, and helps them understand how to cope with their depression.

- Lifestyle changes such as physical exercise may help people who suffer from Depression.

- For some severe forms of Depression, electroconvulsive therapy (ECT) is a safe and effective treatment. It may be lifesaving for people who are psychotic, at high risk of suicide, or who, because of the severity of their illness, have stopped eating or drinking and may die as a result.

For more information on Depression, check out:

**http://issuu.com/weusthem/docs/magazine_
depression/1?e=8480834/6664711**

MODULE 3

Group 4: Understanding Depression

What is Depression?

How common is Depression?

Describe some of the symptoms of Depression:

List and briefly describe some of the main types of Depression:

What type of treatment is available for people experiencing Depression?

What other kinds of support can help a person with Depression recover?

94

Group 5: Eating Disorders

What are Eating Disorders?

Anorexia Nervosa (AN) and Bulimia Nervosa (BN) are the two most common serious eating disorders. Each illness involves a preoccupation with control over body weight, eating and food. Sometimes they occur together.

- People with AN are determined to control the amounts of food they eat
- People with BN tend to feel out of control with food

Anorexia Nervosa may affect up to one in every two hundred teenage girls, although the illness can be experienced earlier and later in life. Most people who have Anorexia Nervosa are female, but males can also develop the disorder.

Bulimia Nervosa may affect up to two in every hundred teenage girls. More females than males develop Bulimia Nervosa.

While these rates show that few people meet the criteria for eating disorders, it is far more common for people to have unrealistic attitudes about body size and shape. These attitudes may contribute to inappropriate eating or dieting practices, such as fad dieting, which is not the same as having an eating disorder.

Both illnesses can be overcome and it is important for the person to seek advice about treatment for either condition as early as possible.

What are the Symptoms of Anorexia Nervosa (AN)?

Anorexia Nervosa is characterized by:

- A loss of at least 15% of body weight resulting from refusal to eat enough food
- Refusal to maintain minimally normal body weight

- An intense fear of becoming 'fat' even though the person is underweight
- Cessation of menstrual periods in girls
- Misperception of body image, so that people see themselves as fat when they're really very thin
- A preoccupation with the preparation of food
- Unusual rituals and activities pertaining to food, such as making lists of 'good' and 'bad' food and hiding food.

Anorexia Nervosa may begin with a weight loss resulting from dieting. Many people diet but only a few develop AN, so clearly dieting does not cause AN. It is not known why some people go on to develop AN while others do not. As weight decreases, the person's ability to appropriately judge their body size and make proper decisions about their eating also decreases.

What are the Symptoms of Bulimia Nervosa (BN)?

Bulimia Nervosa is characterized by:

- Eating binges involve consumption of large amounts of calorie-rich food, during which the person feels a loss of personal control and following which the person feels self disgust
- Attempts to compensate for binges and to avoid weight gain by self-induced vomiting, and/or abuse of laxatives and diuretics
- Strong concerns about body shape and weight

A person with BN is usually average or slightly above average weight for height, so it is often less recognizable than the person with AN.

BN often starts with rigid weight reduction dieting in an attempt to reach 'thinness'. But again, many people diet while only a few develop BN.

Eating Disorders (cont.)

Vomiting after a binge seems to bring a sense of relief, but this is temporary and soon turns to distress and guilt. Some people use laxatives, but these do not cause weight loss. Instead they make it difficult for your body by causing dehydration and poor absorption of vitamins and minerals the body needs.

The person can make many efforts to break from the pattern, but the binge/purge/exercise cycle, and the feelings associated with it, may have become compulsive and uncontrollable.

What Causes Anorexia Nervosa and Bulimia Nervosa?

The causes of AN and BN remain unclear. Biological and social factors may be involved. While there are many hypotheses about various factors involved in AN, there is no good scientific evidence which shows causality for one particular pathway.

What are the Effects of Anorexia Nervosa and Bulimia Nervosa?

Physical effects

The physical effects can be serious, but are often reversible if the illnesses are tackled early. If left untreated, AN and BN can be life-threatening. Responding to early warning signs and obtaining early treatment is essential. AN can lead to death from the physical effects of starvation.

Both illnesses, when severe, can cause:

- Harm to kidneys
- Urinary tract infections and damage to the colon
- Dehydration, constipation and diarrhea
- Seizures, muscle spasms or cramps

- Chronic indigestion
- Loss of menstruation or irregular periods
- Heart palpitations

Many of the effects of AN are related to malnutrition, including:

- Absence of menstrual periods
- Severe sensitivity to cold
- Growth of down-like hair all over the body
- Inability to think rationally and to concentrate

Severe BN is likely to cause:

- Erosion of dental enamel from vomiting
- Swollen salivary glands
- The possibility of a ruptured stomach or esophagus
- Chronic sore throat

Eating Disorders (cont.)

Emotional and Psychological Effects:

These are likely to include

- Difficulty with activities which involve food
- Loneliness, due to self-imposed isolation and a reluctance to develop personal relationships
- Deceptive behaviours related to food
- Fear of the disapproval of others if the illness becomes known, mixed with the hope that family and friends might intervene and offer help
- Mood swings, changes in personality, emotional outbursts or depressive feelings

How can Eating Disorders be Treated?

Changes in eating behaviour may be caused by several illnesses other than AN or BN, so a thorough medical examination by a medical doctor is the first step.

Once the illness has been diagnosed, a range of health providers can be involved in treatment, because the illness affects people both physically and mentally. Professionals involved in treatment may include psychiatrists, psychologists, physicians, dietitians, social workers, occupational therapists and nurses.

Outpatient treatment and attendance in special programs are the preferred method of treatment for people with AN. Hospitalization may be necessary for those who are severely malnourished.

There is no known medication for treating AN. Many people with BN get better taking an antidepressant medicine, even if they do not have Depression.

Dietary education assists with retraining in healthy eating habits.

Counselling and specific therapies such as Cognitive Behavioural Therapy (CBT) are used to help change unhealthy thoughts about eating. The ongoing support of family and friends is essential.

In teenagers, a type of family therapy called Multidimensional Family Therapy is often used.

Group 5: Understanding Eating Disorders

What are eating disorders?

How common are eating disorders?

Describe some of the symptoms of Anorexia Nervosa (AN) and Bulimia Nervosa (BN):

What are some physical, emotional and psychological effects of AN and BN?

What type of treatments are available for people experiencing AN and BN?

What other kinds of support can help people with eating disorders recover?

MODULE 3

Group 6: Schizophrenia

What is Schizophrenia?

Schizophrenia is a mental illness which affects about one person in every hundred. Schizophrenia is of a group of illnesses called Psychotic Disorders. It interferes with a person's mental functioning and behaviour, and in the long term may cause changes to their personality.

The first onset of Schizophrenia is usually in adolescence or early adulthood. Some people may experience only one or more brief episodes of psychosis in their lives, and it may not develop the illness called Schizophrenia. For others, it may remain a recurrent or life-long condition.

The onset of the illness may occasionally be rapid, with acute symptoms developing over months. More commonly, it may be slow, developing over years.

Schizophrenia is characterized by two different sets of symptoms: positive symptoms such as delusions (thinking things that aren't true), or hallucinations (seeing or hearing things that aren't there).

Negative symptoms refer to things that are taken away by the illness, so that a person has less energy, less pleasure and interest in normal life activities, spending less time with friends, being less able to think clearly. These symptoms tend to begin gradually and become more pronounced over years.

What are the Symptoms of Schizophrenia?

Positive symptoms of Schizophrenia include:

Delusions – false beliefs of persecution, guilt or grandeur, or being under outside control. These beliefs will not change regardless of the evidence against them. People with Schizophrenia may describe outside plots against them or think they have special powers or gifts. Sometimes they withdraw from people or hide to avoid imagined persecution.

Hallucinations – most commonly involving hearing voices. Other less common experiences can include seeing, feeling, tasting or smelling things (which to the person are real but which are not actually there).

Thought disorder – where the speech may be difficult to follow, for example, jumping from one subject to another with no logical connection. Thoughts and speech may be jumbled and disjointed. The person may think someone is interfering with their mind.

Other symptoms of Schizophrenia include:

Loss of drive – when the ability to engage in everyday activities (such as washing and cooking) is lost. This lack of drive, initiative or motivation is part of the illness and is not laziness.

Blunted expression of emotions – where the ability to express emotion is reduced and is often accompanied by a lack of response or an inappropriate response to external events such as feeling happy on a sad occasion.

Social withdrawal – this may be caused by a number of factors including the fear that someone is going to harm them, or a fear of interacting with others because of a loss of social skills.

Lack of insight or awareness of other conditions – because some experiences such as delusions or hallucinations are so real, it is common for people with Schizophrenia to be unaware they are ill. For this and other reasons, such as medication side-effects, they may refuse to accept treatment which could be essential for their well being.

Thinking difficulties – a person's concentration, memory and ability to plan and organize may be affected, making it more difficult to reason, communicate and complete daily tasks.

What Causes Schizophrenia?

No single cause has been identified, but several factors are believed to contribute to the onset of Schizophrenia.

Schizophrenia (cont.)

Genetic factors – A predisposition to Schizophrenia can run in families and has a genetic cause. In the general population, about one percent of people develop it over their lifetime. Some people develop the illness without having it in their family.

Family relationships – No evidence has been found to support the suggestion that family relationships cause the illness. However, some people with Schizophrenia are sensitive to family tensions which, for them, may be associated with relapses.

Environment – It is considered that stressful incidents often precede the diagnosis of Schizophrenia; they can act as precipitating events in vulnerable people. People with Schizophrenia often become anxious, irritable and unable to concentrate before any acute symptoms are evident. This can cause relationships to deteriorate, possibly leading to divorce or unemployment. Often these factors are blamed for the onset of the illness when, in fact, the illness itself has caused the crisis. There is some evidence that environmental factors that damage brain development (such as a viral illness in utero) may lead to Schizophrenia later in life.

Drug use – The use of some drugs, such as cannabis (marijuana), LSD, Crack and crystal meth is likely to cause a relapse in Schizophrenia. Some people with a particular genetic type may be at higher risk for Schizophrenia if they us marijuana often. Occasionally, severe drug use may lead to or "unmask" Schizophrenia.

Myths, Misunderstandings and Facts

Myths, misunderstandings, negative stereotypes and attitudes surround the issue of mental illness in general - and in particular, Schizophrenia. They result in stigma, discrimination and isolation.

Do people with Schizophrenia have a split personality?

No. Schizophrenia refers to the change in the person's mental function where the thoughts and perceptions become disordered.

Are people with Schizophrenia intellectually disabled?

No. The illness is not an intellectual disability.

Are people with Schizophrenia dangerous?

Not mostly. People with Schizophrenia are generally not dangerous when receiving appropriate treatment. However, a minority of people with the illness may become aggressive when experiencing an untreated acute episode, or if they are taking illicit drugs. This is usually expressed to family and friends - rarely to strangers.

Is Schizophrenia a life-long mental disorder?

Like many mental illnesses, Schizophrenia is usually lifelong. However, most people, with professional help and social support, learn to manage their symptoms and have a satisfactory quality of life. About 20-30 percent of people with Schizophrenia have only one or two psychotic episodes in their lives.

How can Schizophrenia be Treated?

The most effective treatment for Schizophrenia involves medication. In addition, psychological counseling and help with managing its impact on everyday life is often needed.

The sooner that Schizophrenia is treated, the better the long-term prognosis or outcome. The opposite is also true: the longer Schizophrenia is left untreated, and the more psychotic breaks are experienced by someone with the illness, the lower the level of eventual recovery. Early intervention is key to helping people recover.

Schizophrenia (cont.)

How can Schizophrenia be Treated? (cont.)

The development of antipsychotic medications has revolutionized the treatment of Schizophrenia. Now, most people can be treated and remain in the community instead of in hospital.

Antipsychotic medications work by correcting the brain chemistry associated with the illness. New medications are emerging which may promote a more complete recovery with fewer side effects than the older versions.

Schizophrenia is an illness like many physical illnesses. Just as insulin is a lifeline for people with diabetes, antipsychotic medications can be a lifeline for a person with Schizophrenia. Just as with diabetes, some people will need to take medication indefinitely to prevent a relapse and keep symptoms under control.

Though there is no known cure for Schizophrenia, regular contact with a doctor or psychiatrist and other mental health professionals such as nurses, occupational therapists and psychologists can help a person with Schizophrenia recover and get on with their lives. Informal supports such as self-help and social support are also very important to recovery. Meaningful activity or employment, and adequate housing and income are all essential to keeping people healthy.

Sometimes specific therapies directed toward symptoms such as delusions may also be useful.

Counselling and social support can help people with Schizophrenia overcome problems with finances, housing, work, socializing and interpersonal relationships.

With effective treatment and support, most people with Schizophrenia can lead fulfilling and productive lives.

MODULE 3

Group 6: Understanding Schizophrenia

What is Schizophrenia?

How common is Schizophrenia?

Describe some of the symptoms of Schizophrenia:

List and briefly explain some of the factors that may contribute to the onset of Schizophrenia:

What type of treatment is available for people with Schizophrenia?

What other kinds of support can help people with Schizophrenia recover?

Group 7: Obsessive Compulsive Disorder (OCD)

What is OCD?

Obsessive Compulsive Disorder is a disturbance of specific brain circuits that leads to two different but related symptoms called "obsessions" and "compulsions". In OCD a person experiences persistent, recurrent, intrusive and unwanted thoughts, ideas or fears (obsessions) and repeated, ritualized behaviours (compulsions) that are done to try and stop the worry and anxiety brought on by the obsessions.

Obsessions are frequent, persistent, recurring thoughts that the person wants to get rid of but can't. These thoughts are so pervasive that they can take over a person's life, constantly intruding into and disrupting every-day activities. The person does not really believe that the thoughts are true but has great difficulty in stopping them. These recurring thoughts cause significant worry and anxiety and may lead to compulsions. Obsessive thoughts commonly involve contamination (there are germs on my hands and I will catch a horrible disease) or harm (my brother will die).

Compulsions are the persistent repetitive rituals that a person does to try and obtain relief from the obsession. Common compulsions include: ordering, washing, counting, tapping, and repeating. These compulsions can take many hours in a day to perform and a person experiencing them frequently feels a strong urge to do them even thought they do not want to.

Although OCD can begin at many different points in a person's life, most commonly it starts before age 20. About 2-3 percent of the population will experience OCD during their lifetime.

Everybody experiences occasional repetitive thoughts, phrases, worries (such as: did I lock the door) or even musical snippets (called "ear worms"). These are normal and are not obsessions. Everyone also experiences occasional repetitive behaviours such as checking to make sure the door is locked or the stove is turned off (even though they know it is). These are not compulsions.

What Causes OCD?

We think that a combination of different things, including genetics and environmental factors lead to OCD. One recently discovered environmental factor is a bacterial infection that leads to an immune reaction involving the brain circuits that are involved in OCD.

How can OCD be Treated?

A number of good treatments are available for OCD. These include both biological and psychological treatments. The Serotonin Specific Reuptake Inhibitors (SSRI) medicines and Cognitive Behavioural Therapy (CBT) are prescribed together to help treat the person that has OCD. Sometimes family therapy is provided because having OCD can affect how a person's family is doing.

A person with OCD can also do a number of other things to try and help. These include exercise and activities that require intensive concentration. While these can be somewhat helpful, they do not take the place of SSRI and CBT treatments.

Group 7: Understanding Obsessive Compulsive Disorder (OCD)

What is OCD?

How common is OCD?

Describe some of the symptoms of OCD:

What combination of factors is thought to cause OCD?

What type of treatment is available for people with OCD?

What other kinds of support can help people with OCD recover?

Group 8: Post-Traumatic Stress Disorder (PTSD)

What is Post-Traumatic Stress Disorder (PTSD)?

PTSD is a disturbance of the normal stress response to a severe and often life-threatening event. This response persists well beyond the expected time and causes significant problems in daily life. Sometimes the PTSD can be so intense that a person has great difficulties at home, work or school and may require a brief period of time in hospital to help recover.

Everyone experiences substantial symptoms of emotional distress when faced with a severe and sometimes life-threatening stressor (such as: being in an automobile accident, being raped, witnessing a murder or an event where people die, experiencing an earthquake, etc.). These symptoms include: anxiety, fear, trouble sleeping, bad dreams, recurring thoughts or images of the event, irritability, etc. These symptoms are normal; everyone who lives through such an experience has them. This is not PTSD. It is called an Acute Stress Reaction (ASR) and it gradually goes away over a few months if the person is in a safe environment and receives support from his/her family and friends.

PTSD is the continuation of the ASR for many months or even years, and also includes other symptoms such as: re-experiencing the event, persistent high emotional intensity, feeling of "being on edge", nightmares, depressed mood and even suicidal thoughts. Fortunately, the majority of people who experience severe and sometimes life-threatening events do not develop PTSD - in fact, most don't.

What Causes PTSD?

Unlike all other mental illnesses, PTSD is ALWAYS caused by a terrible event that occurs in a person's life. However, most people who experience such events do not develop PTSD. Recently scientists have discovered that genes also play an important role in determining who will and who will not develop PTSD.

How can PTSD be Treated?

PTSD is usually diagnosed if severe symptoms that negatively impact daily life have persisted for months after the event. A number of psychological treatments can be prescribed and can be helpful for many people. Some people with PTSD will also benefit from taking one of a number of different medications. We also know that some things we do for people after they experience a traumatic event can increase the risk that they will get PTSD. These things include forcing people to talk about the event after they have experienced it in the mistaken belief that forcing them to talk about it will make it better for them.

Support from family members, friends and the wider community are helpful for people who have PTSD. As with all mental disorders, taking care of your physical health by getting enough exercise, eating healthy foods, limiting use of alcohol, avoiding drugs and being with people who care for you can provide additional benefit to prescribed treatments.

Group 8: Understanding Post-Traumatic Stress Disorder (PTSD)

What is PTSD?

How common is PTSD?

Describe some of the symptoms of PTSD:

What combination of factors is thought to cause PTSD?

What type of treatment is available for people with PTSD?

What other kinds of support can help people with PTSD recover?

MODULE 3

Activity 4: (10 mins.)

Sharing the Pieces

Purpose:

- In this activity, the "student experts" will share their new knowledge about their mental illness with others in the class. In this way, each student will gain an increased understanding of the mental illnesses covered in the unit.

How-to:

1) Form new, mixed groups which include at least one member from each of the illness-specific groups.

2) Give each student two minutes to report to the newly-formed group about their specific area of mental illness, highlighting important points about how common the illness is, symptoms and effective supports and treatments.

Parents and Mental Illness

Some of your students will have a parent or other family member (including a sibling) who has a mental illness. Information about how to better deal with the experience of having a parent or sibling with a mental illness is now available at **www.teenmentalhealth.org/toolbox**. Please bring the "Family Pack" to the attention of your students by showing the class where they can find it.

MODULE 4 PREPARATION

Experiences of Mental Illness

Overview

In this module students will hear directly from other young people about their personal experiences with mental illness. In their own words, a number of young people describe their symptoms, the difficulties they went through as a result of their illness, and how the illness affected their lives at school, within their families, and in their friendships.

Students will work together in small groups to explore the impact of mental illnesses on the lives of the young people in the video.

Learning Objectives

- To recognize, on a more personal level, the way mental illnesses can impact on a person's life
- To appreciate the importance of getting help and proper treatment

Major Concepts Addressed

- Mental illnesses are diseases that affect many aspects of a person's life
- While they are usually lifelong, mental illnesses are often episodic and with effective treatment, most people can function well in everyday life

Teacher Background and Preparation

Teachers should preview Module 4 materials and each of the six video stories. Reviewing the videos in advance will help you become familiar with the content so that you can then help students understand how a mental illness has affected the lives of these youth.

The materials are located on:
http://teenmentalhealth.org/curriculum/modules/module-4/

The password is: **t33nh3alth**

MODULE 4

Activities

- Activity 1:   Experiences of Mental Illness Video and Discussion Sheet (40 mins.)

In Advance

- Decide whether you will show the videos to the class as a whole or you want smaller groups to view the videos through the web-based format
- Set up computer work stations
- Photocopy Activity 1 Video discussion sheet (1 copy of each per student)

Materials Required

- Web-based videos
- Handout: Activity 1 Video discussion sheet

MODULE 4

V

Discussion of the video may raise the issue of youth suicide. While this discussion is appropriate within the broader context of mental illness, it is important that the discussion not become focused on suicide. Any discussion of suicide should:

- avoid portraying suicide as romantic, heroic or tragic;

- avoid increasing knowledge about methods of suicide;

- emphasize the importance of seeking help and of everyone's responsibility to tell a trusted adult if a friend mentions thoughts of suicide, even if that person asks for it to be kept a secret.

Activity 1: (40 mins.)

Experiences of Mental Illness Video and Discussion Sheet

Purpose:

- To explore the impact of mental illnesses on a young person.

- To look specifically at the experience of each character in the video through small group work.

How-to:

1) Inform the class that the videos they are about to see were created by young people who have experienced mental illness, and that they are about their experiences.

   Before showing the videos, divide the class into 6 groups and distribute the video activity sheet. Allocate each group one of the videos.

   Give the students a few minutes to read through the questions on the video discussion sheet. Explain that each group will focus specifically on one video.

2) Each group should play their video.

3) While in their small groups and after watching the video, have each group member complete his/her discussion sheet. After everyone has completed their own discussion sheet ask each group to talk about what they have written and to create a single group discussion sheet that one of the group members will then share with the class as a whole.

4) Bring the groups back together and ask a member of each group to summarize the discussion from each of the small groups for the class.

Suicidal Thoughts

Thoughts about suicide are common in adolescents. However, persistent or recurring thoughts about suicide signal that help is needed. It is useful to make sure your students understand that persistent or recurring thoughts about suicide is a signal to them that they need some extra help, and if they are experiencing this they should talk to the school counselor.

110

V

The most important concept for students to grasp through the class discussion is that although the individuals in the video had different mental illnesses and different experiences, there are some common themes and concerns for each person. Prompt students to think about the similarities among the individuals that are brought up.

How-to (cont.):

5) Using the questions below, facilitate a discussion with the whole class:

    a) What specific illnesses were mentioned in the videos?

    b) What help or treatment did the people receive?

    c) Did the people recover?

    d) What did they find helpful to help them recover?

6) Conclude the activity by addressing any questions that students may have after watching the videos.

In Class Personal Contacts

Some schools have organizations (such as the Canadian Mental Health Organization) that have trained and professionally supported youth speakers that can provide personal experiences about their mental disorder. If such a resource is available in your community, this module provides an excellent opportunity to take advantage of that. Make sure that a reputable organization, a trained youth speaker and psychological supports are available to the speaker. Do not invite speakers who do not meet all three criteria. Speakers should not focus on self-harm or suicide.

Video Discussion Sheet

What are some of the symptoms of the illness that are described?

How did the illness affect the person?

Did the illness cause the person difficulty in his or her life? In what ways?

What kind of treatment did the person get?

What kinds of things have helped the person recover and stay well?

What questions would you like to ask the person in the video in order to better understand their illness?

MODULE 5

Seeking Help and Finding Support

Overview

How do we decide that what a person is experiencing is outside the range of the normal ups and downs we all go through? When is it time to seek assistance from health providers?

Seeking help and finding support for mental health problems or mental illness can be a tricky business. From the outside, it's often not clear when intervention is necessary, and people who are experiencing a mental illness may themselves not always be aware of what's going on, and can be reluctant to come forward for fear of being stigmatized.

When people know that they will not be stigmatized, they are more likely to seek help. Early intervention is important and increases the chances of recovery.

This lesson will address the issues around help seeking, as well as providing ideas about ways in which that help and support can be accessed - within the school and beyond.

Learning Objectives

- To understand that people may need support to deal with some very stressful life events and situations

- To learn to distinguish between "normal" responses to stress and those that may indicate a need for additional support from health professionals

- To get students to consider who they could talk to if they were worried about their own mental health, or that of a friend or relative

- To identify support personnel in the school relevant to mental health

- To become familiar with the range of community-based healthcare services and groups available to support people who are experiencing mental illness and their families and friends

Major Concepts Addressed

- Mental illnesses, like chronic physical illnesses, can be effectively treated

- Stigma acts as a barrier to people seeking help for mental illness

- Getting help early increases the chances that a person will make a full recovery from mental illness

- Recovery from mental illness is possible when a range of evidence based treatments and supports are available

Teacher Background and Preparation

- Read through all activities and handouts before class

- Preview PowerPoint: Treatment and Recovery

- Compile list of community mental health resources for students

MODULE 5

Activities

- Activity 1: PowerPoint Presentation: Treatment and Recovery (15 mins.)
- Activity 2: Getting Help (15 mins.)
- Activity 3: My Questions (15 mins.)
- Activity 4: Support Strategies (10 mins.)

In Advance

- Fill out Community Mental Health Resources list for your class (page 162)
- Preview PowerPoint
- Set up computer(s) to view PowerPoint
- Prepare cards

Online Supplementary Materials

The supplementary materials are designed to enable you to challenge students in your class to learn more about different mental disorders. These may or may not be resources you wish to employ. Please review them and decide if and how you wish to use them.

If you are also using Teacher Knowledge Update, print as many copies as you think will be necessary for your class.

Useful Links

Here to Help, BC
http://www.heretohelp.bc.ca/

Michael Chan EMental Health:
http://www.ementalhealth.ca

MyHealth Magazine:
http://www.myhealthmagazine.net/

Support programs by National Alliance on Mental Illness (NAMI):
http://www.nami.org/Template.cfm?section=Find_Support

Sun Life Financial Chair in Adolescent Mental Health:
http://www.teenmentalhealth.org/toolbox/family-pack

The Self-Help Resource Centre of Ontario:
http://www.selfhelp.on.ca/

Youth Engagement:
http://www.jcsh-cces.ca/ye-book

MODULE 5

Template - Community Mental Health Resources

The following mental health related resources are available in many communities including youth oriented programs. Find out the contact information for these resources in your community and distribute to students. Your local Canadian Mental Health Association branch can provide assistance.

School Resources:

- Guidance counselor
- Social worker
- Nurse
- Peer support

Local Community Resources:

- Crisis/distress lines
- Mental health lines
- Youth centres
- Drop-ins
- Community health centres
- Hospitals/clinics
- First episode centres
- Peer support groups

Mental Health Information (National):

- Canadian Mental Health Association (www.cmha.ca)
- Centre for Addiction and Mental Health (www.camh.net)
- Mood Disorders Society of Canada (www.mooddisorderscanada.ca)
- Schizophrenia Society of Canada (www.schizophrenia.ca)
- Anxiety Disorders Association of Canada (www.anxietycanada.ca)
- Teen Mental Health (www.teenmentalhealth.org)

Kids Help Phone (www.kidshelppphone.ca) – 1-800-668-6868

Kids Help Phone is Canada's only 24-hour, national bilingual telephone counseling service for children and youth. It provides counseling to children and youth directly between the ages of 4 and 19 years and helps adults aged 20 and over to find the counseling services they need.

MODULE 5

Activity 1: (15 mins.)

PowerPoint Presentation:
Treatment and Recovery

Purpose:

- The PowerPoint "Treatments and Recovery" discusses what treatments are available and what they do (as well as what recovery means).
- Students should understand that most mental disorders can be effectively treated and help-seeking is the key to recovery.

How-to:

1) Use the web version of the presentation by logging on to:

http://teenmentalhealth.org/curriculum/wp-content/uploads/2015/05/April2015_Module-5-PP.compressed-1.pdf

The password is: **t33nh3alth**

MODULE 5

V

Remind students that communicating their concerns about coping and dealing with mental health and other difficulties is really hard, and takes a lot of courage.

It's a good idea to anticipate potential student disclosures and to be prepared to deal properly with these situations. Ask the school social worker to be on hand if possible.

Activity 2: (15 mins.)

Getting Help

Purpose:

- To describe a range of scenarios in which it would be important to tell or refer a problem to an appropriate adult.

How-to:

1) Explain to students that they will be engaging in a problem-solving lesson in which they can speculate about the possible actions they could take in a range of situations involving young people in distress. They will explore the scenarios using a game.

2) Ask students to arrange themselves into groups of four to six. Get them to sit in a circle (on the floor might be easiest).

3) Hand out the set of cards from the Activity Sheet: What if… scenarios. Ask each group to lay out their What if… cards in a circle with enough room inside the circle to spin a bottle or pen.

4) In turn, each of the participants takes a spin, and read out the card the bottle points to. The person whose turn it is speculates first about what to do in such a situation, then others help out by adding their views, questions or challenges.

5) When they have finished discussing the scenarios, ask the class to come back together and pose the following questions:

- Was there any disagreement in the groups about what was best to do?

- Which was the scenario most likely to actually happen out of those you discussed?

- Which do you think would be the hardest scenario to deal with if it happened to you or a friend or family member?

- What sorts of fears or concerns would stop people from seeking help or telling someone else in these situations?

- What kinds of things would motivate someone to seek help or tell someone their concerns in the situations you discussed?

6) Distribute "Something's not quite right" checklists and read them through with the class.

MODULE 5

What if.........Scenarios

1 Your friend seems really down and talks about dropping out of school.

2 A friend has been on a diet, is getting really skinny and never seems to eat. She thinks she's really fat and will not wear shorts or a bathing suit.

3 Since your dad left, your brother/sister is spending almost all of their time smoking, drinking and watching TV, and never wanting to do anything else. You have not told your friends about your parents splitting up.

4 There is a situation at school that is really stressing you out. Everyday when you wake up, you remember the situation and start to feel sick.

5 Your friend says s/he would be better off if s/he ran away. Your friend has already been sleeping over at your house a lot lately.

6 Someone in your class has started smoking marijuana before school everyday. The friends who smoke with this person only do it occasionally on the weekends. People are joking about how s/he is behaving – out of it and spacey. The person seems pretty down to you.

7 Your friend has started taking different kinds of pills at school, and is asking other people for painkillers all the time.

8 Your friend isn't acting like his old self. He seems really down, and has been doing strange things like giving his favourite things away. He recently told you that he thought that people he knew would be better off without him around, and that he'd thought about killing himself. After he tells you, he asks you not to tell anyone else about what he's said.

9 A kid in your class often gets completely ignored and occasionally teased and even bullied. No one will ever be seen talking to this person. The teachers don't seem to notice, and no one does anything to this kid when teachers are around.

10 A friend has started skipping a lot of school and seems pretty down.

11 Your friend has a parent with mental illness. From time to time, when the parent isn't doing well, your friend has to do everything at home. None of your other friends know about the situation. Your friend doesn't even know that you know. Your mom found out through a neighbour.

12 A classmate who is not really your friend, but is not friends with anyone else either, has started acting really strangely. Other kids have been laughing and making fun of them, but underneath you think this is a bit scary, and maybe the person is not doing this on purpose.

Something is Not Quite Right: Getting Help Early for Mental Illness

You have a feeling that something is "not quite right" about the way someone close to you is behaving. You're worried, but you're not sure if it might be serious, or if moodiness, irritability and withdrawn behaviour is a stage they'll grow out of. Could drugs be involved? Do you think you might need a professional opinion to help you decide if there is a serious problem?

Getting help early

The chances are that there is not a serious problem, and that time, reassurance and support are all that are needed. However, if a mental illness is developing, then getting help early is very important.

Being unwell for a shorter time means less time lost as school or work and more time for relationships, experiences and activities which help us stay emotionally healthy.

Checklist #1 Difficult behaviour at home, at school or in the workplace:

Behaviour which is considered "normal", although difficult:

People may be:

☐ rude ☐ weepy ☐ thoughtless ☐ irritable ☐ argumentative ☐ over-sensitive

☐ over-emotional ☐ lazy ☐ withdrawn ☐ rebellious ☐ shy

These behaviours may also occur as a normal, brief reaction to stressful events such as:

☐ breakup of a close relationship ☐ moving ☐ divorce ☐ other family crisis

☐ death of a loved one ☐ other personal crisis ☐ exam failure ☐ physical illness

Probably no cause for serious concern, but…

It is often best to try not to over-react. Try to be as supportive as possible while waiting for the "bad patch" to pass. If the behaviour is too disruptive or is distressing to other people, or if the difficult behaviour lasts a long time, then you could seek professional counseling, help or advice. Talk it over with your family doctor, school counselor, community or mental health centre.

MODULE 5

Activity 2
HANDOUT

Checklist #2 – What's the difference between just having a bad day and something potentially more serious?

Signs of Clinical Depression:

☐ Feeling sad and miserable for at least 2 weeks, most of the day, everyday

☐ Feeling like crying a lot of the time

☐ Not wanting to do anything, go anywhere, see anyone

☐ Having trouble concentrating or getting things done

☐ Feeling like you're operating in "slow-motion"

☐ Having trouble sleeping

☐ Feeling tired and lacking energy – being unable to get out of bed even after a full night's sleep

☐ Having a change in appetite, usually a loss of appetite

☐ Feeling hopeless

☐ Thinking of suicide

☐ Always putting yourself down and thinking you're no good or that nothing really matters

If you often experience a number of these things - you may have Depression. Remember that you don't have to be alone with these feelings, and that Depression is treatable!

120

Adapted from *MindMatters: Understanding Mental Illness*, Pg. 77-79

Checklist #3 – Behaviours which are considered ABNORMAL for that person, and may seriously affect other people.

People may:	
☐ Withdraw completely from family, friends, and workmates	☐ Lose variation in mood – be "flat" – lack emotional expression, for example, humour or friendliness
☐ Be afraid to leave the house (particularly during daylight hours)	☐ Have marked changes in mood, from quiet to excited or agitated
☐ Sleep or eat poorly	☐ Hear voices that no one else can hear
☐ Sleep by day and stay awake at night, often pacing restlessly	☐ Believe, without reason, that others are plotting against, spying on, or following them, and be extremely angry or afraid of these people
☐ Be extremely occupied with a particular theme, for example, death, politics or religion	☐ Believe that they are being harmed or asked to do things against their will, by, for instance, television, radio, aliens, God or the devil
☐ Uncharacteristically neglect household or parental responsibilities, or personal appearance or hygiene	☐ Believe they have special powers, for example, that they are important religious leaders, politicians or scientists
☐ Deteriorate in performance at school or work	
☐ Have difficulty concentrating, following conversation or remembering things	☐ Believe that their thoughts are being interfered with or that they can influence the thoughts of others
☐ Talk about or write things that do not really make sense	☐ Spend extravagant or unrealistic sums of money
☐ Panic, be extremely anxious, or significantly depressed and suicidal	

Seek medical assessment as soon as possible. These types of behaviours are much clearer signs that someone needs to be checked out, particularly if they have been present for several weeks. They may be only a minor disturbance, but a mental illness such as a psychotic disorder may be developing.

MODULE 5

Activity 3: (15 mins.)

My Questions

Purpose:

- To provide each student with a number of questions that they should routinely use when they discuss recommended treatment with their health provider.

How-to:

1) Direct the students to **http://teenmentalhealth.org/toolbox/communicating-health-care-provider-every-person-ask/**. Have them download or print the resource there.

2) Ask each student to carefully read the document and choose one or two questions from each category that they would like to use as their "go-to" questions when visiting a health care provider.

3) Have each student create their own personal "My Questions" file and save it to their preferred electronic device.

MODULE 5

V

Make sure to emphasize that everyone has a personal responsibility to take action if a friend mentions thoughts of suicide. Young people should always share this information with a trusted adult – like a teacher, guidance counselor, coach, relative or parent – and never promise to keep the information secret.

Activity 4: (10 mins.)

Support Strategies

Purpose:

- To provide students with strategies for supporting friends and others who are having trouble coping because of mental health problems or mental illness.

How-to:

1) Begin a discussion about the role that young people often play as supporters when they listen to their friends talk about their problems.

   Ask students how they would like to be treated if they had a mental illness. Use the overhead as a starting point to encourage further discussion. Distribute photocopies of Activity 4 Support strategies and Recovery: What works? to each student. Read through the sheets with the class.

Support Strategies

Here are some strategies for supporting someone with a mental health problem/illness:

- Be supportive and understanding.

- Spend time with the person. Listen to him or her.

- Never underestimate the person's capacity to recover.

- Encourage the person to follow his or her treatment plan and to seek out support services. Offer to accompany them to appointments.

- Become informed about mental illness.

- Remember that even though your friend may be going through a hard time they will recover. Stand by them.

- If you're planning an outing to the movies or the community centre, remember to ask your friend along. Keeping busy and staying in touch with friends will help your friend feel better, when they're ready.

- If you are a close friend or family member of someone who has a mental illness, make sure you get support as well. Crisis training, self-help and/or individual counseling will help you become a better support person.

- Put the person's life before your friendship. If you think the person needs help, especially if he or she mentions thoughts of suicide, don't keep it a secret – even if the person asked you to.

> If a friend mentions thoughts of suicide or self-harm, you NEED to tell his or her parents, a teacher, guidance counselor or someone else who can help. It's better to have a friend who's angry with you for a while than to keep their secret and live with knowing you could have helped but remained quiet when your friend was in trouble.

Recovery – What Helps People With Mental Illness Get (and Stay) Better?

Recovery is an ongoing, slow process, and is different for each person. Research on recovery shows that there are a number of factors which people often mention are important:

- The presence of people who believe in and stand by the person who is in recovery.

- That person's ability to make their own choices about important things like treatment and housing.

Other factors that can support recovery include:

- Mutual support (self-help groups)

- Social opportunities (church groups, drop-in centres, volunteer work, participating in community life)

- Positive relationships (accepting and being accepted, family and friends and communicating with them in a positive way)

- Meaningful daily activity - being able to work, go to school

- Medication (sticking with a treatment plan, working with doctors to find the best medications with the fewest side effects)

- Spirituality (involvement in a faith community or individual spiritual practice)

- Inner healing capacity and inner peace (finding a sense of meaning and purpose, even in suffering)

- Personal growth and development (hobbies, self education, taking control of one's life, exercise, personal goal setting)

- Self-awareness (self-monitoring, recognizing when to seek help, recognizing one's accomplishments and accepting and/or learning from one's failures)

Deegan et. al., 2000, Canadian Mental Health Association, NS Division 1995

The Importance of Positive Mental Health

Overview

What constitutes a mentally healthy person? Does everyone have mental health? In this module, students will explore these questions and will look at the impact of mental health on overall well-being. Through several group activities, students will also learn about the impact of stress, and will identify appropriate and effective coping strategies to deal with stress.

Learning Objectives

- To describe the characteristics of an emotionally healthy person
- To learn about and demonstrate skills that enhance personal mental health, including stress management techniques

Major Concepts Addressed

- Everyone has mental health that can be supported and promoted - regardless of whether or not they also have a mental illness
- Positive coping strategies can help everyone maintain and enhance their mental mealth

Teacher Preparation

Read through all activities before class.

Activities

- Activity 1: Taking Care of Your Mental Health (5 mins.)
- Activity 2: What Do We Mean By "Stress?" (15 mins.)
- Activity 3: How Do You Cope? (15 mins.)
- Activity 4: Taking Charge of My Health (15 mins.)
- Activity 5: How Do I Teen My Parent? and How Do I Parent My Teen? (15 mins.)

In Advance

- Photocopy handouts for Activity 1: Taking Care of Your Mental Health (one copy for each student) and Activity 3: Coping Cards (only one copy)
- Cut out Coping Cards
- Copy Activity 4 "Taking Charge of my Health" – one copy per student

126

MODULE 6

Materials Required

- Handouts: Activity 1: Taking Care of Your Mental Health and Activity 3: Coping Cards
- Flip chart, paper and pens

Online Supplementary Materials

The supplementary materials are designed to enable you to challenge students in your class to learn more about different mental disorders. These may or may not be resources you wish to employ. Please review them and decide if and how you wish to use them.

If you are also using Teacher Knowledge Update, print as many copies as you think will be necessary for your class.

Useful Links

Dr. Dan Siegel: The Healthy Mind Platter
http://www.drdansiegel.com/resources/healthy_mind_platter/

JCSH
http://jcsh-cces.ca

MODULE 6

www.teenmentalhealth. org and **www. keltymentalhealth.ca** are trusted resources for youth mental health. Other potential useful websites are listed in the resources section of this guide.

Activity 1: (5 mins.)

Taking Care of Your Mental Health

Purpose:

- To explore students' growing understanding of mental health, and its importance to themselves.
- To brainstorm about the kinds of things that contribute to positive mental health.

How-to:

1) Ask students to brainstorm ideas of the kinds of things that keep people mentally healthy. Potential ideas are listed below:

- think positive
- organize your time
- value yourself
- eat right and exercise
- try new things
- get enough sleep
- make plans
- set realistic goals and work towards them
- reward yourself
- share concerns and worries with friends and family

2) Hand out photocopies of 'Taking care of your mental health' for students to keep.

The Importance of Good Mental Health:

Achieving mental health is about striking a balance in the social, physical, spiritual, economic and mental aspects of our lives. Reaching a balance is a learning process and it is ongoing. At times, we may tip the balance too much in one direction and have to find our footing again. Our personal balance is highly individual, and our challenge is to stay mentally healthy by finding and keeping that balance.

To find out more about building healthy self-esteem, creating positive relationships, coping with change, and learning to manage stress, read the 10 tips below taken from the CMHA fact sheet Mental Health For Life at **www.ontario.cmha.ca/ fact_sheets.asp?cID=3219**.

From nurturing relationships with family and friends, to identifying and dealing with situations that upset you – including stressful circumstances such as the pressure of exams, a conflict at work, or a misunderstanding with a friend – you can take steps to improve and maintain your mental health throughout your life.

The Canadian Mental Health Association has <u>10 tips for mental health</u>:

1. Build a healthy self-esteem
2. Receive as well as give
3. Create positive parenting and family relationships
4. Make friends who count
5. Figure out your priorities
6. Get involved
7. Learn to manage stress effectively
8. Cope with changes that affect you
9. Deal with your emotions
10. Have a spirituality to call your own

MODULE 6

Taking Care of Your Mental Health

Consider these key characteristics when assessing your own mental health:

You can gauge your mental health by thinking about how you coped with a recent difficulty. Did you feel there was no way out of the problem and that life would never be normal again? Were you unable to carry on with work or school? With time, were you able to enjoy your life, family and friendships? Were you able to regain your balance and look forward to the future?

Taking the pulse of mental health brings different results for everyone; it's unique to each individual. By reflecting on these characteristics, you can recognize your strengths and identify areas where your level of mental fitness could be improved.

Ability to enjoy life – Can you live in the moment and appreciate the "now"? Are you able to learn from the past and plan for the future without dwelling on things you can't change or predict?

Resilience – Are you able to bounce back from hard times? Can you manage the stress of a serious life event without losing your optimism and sense of perspective?

Balance – Are you able to juggle the many aspects of your life? Can you recognize when you might be devoting too much time to one aspect, at the expense of others? Are you able to make changes to restore balance when necessary?

Self-actualization – Do you recognize and develop your strengths so that you can reach your full potential?

Flexibility – Do you feel (and express) a range of emotions? When problems arise, can you change your expectations – of life, others, yourself – to solve the problem and feel better?

Stress is often good for you. Stress has a powerful adaptive function. It helps us solve problems, create new ideas and learn new skills. Too little stress stifles creativity. Too much stress can immobilize us. We need the right amount of stress for success.

MODULE 6

Activity 2: (15 mins.)

What Do We Mean By "Stress?"

Purpose:

- To identify different kinds of stress and the impact that stress can have on overall well-being.

- To give examples of stressors commonly experienced by young people, and explore different coping strategies and positive ways of dealing with stress.

How-to:

1) Ask students to imagine that they are about to explain to an alien what human beings mean by stress. Ask them to form pairs and talk with their partner and develop a definition (e.g. "stress is when…") and write their ideas down in point form.

2) Ask each pair to share their definitions, and write them on the board as they read them aloud.

3) Ask students what they notice about what stress means to different people.

4) Ask students to brainstorm about the different kinds of stressors. Use the list below as a guide to make sure all areas are mentioned. Write their responses on the board.

   Different kinds of stressors:

   - Physical stressors (e.g. injury, illness, fatigue, hunger, lack of shelter)
   - Social stressors (e.g. arguments, rejection, embarrassment)
   - Intellectual stressors (e.g. mental fatigue, lack of understanding)
   - Emotional stressors (e.g. death of a close friend or family member)
   - Spiritual Stressors (e.g. guilt, moral conflicts, lack of sense of purpose)

MODULE 6

V

Introduce the idea that stress can be seen either as a challenge or an opportunity, or as a nightmare or trap. Tell students that people who can imagine or visualize themselves handling their challenges or stresses in a positive way, with an image of themselves having some power or control, are able to bounce back more easily after difficult times. Provide the example of professional athletes, who often use mental pictures to visualize themselves conquering a challenge. Explain to students that this technique can also work for the rest of us – that we can all work at inventing or imagining pictures of ourselves succeeding, and this can help us to do our best in a situation where we fear failure, embarrassment or hard work. Explain that research has shown that people who can learn to visualize themselves succeeding are more likely to actually succeed.

Activity 2: (15 mins.)

What Do We Mean By "Stress?" (cont.)

How-to (cont.):

5) Divide students into groups of four or five. Ask each group to brainstorm around the following question: "What are some of the stresses and challenges people around your age face?"

Circulate around the room as the students are brainstorming in their groups, and use the probes below if they need help or direction:

- What sorts of stresses in the physical environment can directly affect how you feel either physically or emotionally?

- What sorts of stresses or challenges can happen to relationships or between people?

- What kinds of happenings or events can cause stress (e.g. family breakup, transitions like leaving school or moving, illness, end of a close relationship, etc.)

- What are some of the fears, anxieties or thoughts that can get people feeling stressed?

6) As the groups report back, ask several students to record the brainstorm results on flip chart paper. Explain that this list will be used later in the next activity.

MODULE 6

Activity 3: (15 mins.)

How Do You Cope?

Purpose:

- To describe a range of coping strategies to deal with stressful and challenging situations.

- To identify some of students' own preferred coping strategies, and examine the effectiveness of different strategies.

How-to:

1) Remind students that in the previous activity they identified the kinds of things people can feel stressed out about, and some of the thoughts and feelings they can have when faced with challenging and stressful situations.

2) Ask students to get into pairs or groups of three, and ask them to share examples of things they like to do when they feel stressed or overworked. Ask a student in each group to write down at least one of the coping strategies discussed. To prepare for the next part of the activity, while students are busy in their groups, stick up one piece of paper in each corner of the room, with the words "Helpful", "Not much use", Useless" and "Harmful" written on them.

3) Explain to the class that in this activity you'll be examining coping strategies, or things that people do in response to stress or challenge. Point out that there is a huge range of possible coping strategies, that it's different for each individual, varies in terms of a person's culture, religious background, gender, etc. and that there is no one right way of coping. Explain that people who cope effectively often have a whole range of different strategies that they use, and that people often learn about coping by watching what their friends and family do.

4) Have students come back together and arrange themselves in a circle. Ask those who recorded their group's coping strategies to put the paper on the floor in the middle of the circle, and spread Coping Cards into the pile, face down. Ask each student to choose two cards or strategies offered by the students.

5) Ask students to choose one of the cards and hold it up at chest height so that it can be read by others.

MODULE 6

How Do You Cope? (cont.)

How-to (cont.):

6) Explain to the class that you will describe a situation of potential stress or challenge. Students will then be asked to move to a defined area of the room according to whether they think their coping strategy would be helpful, not much use, useless or harmful.

7) Describe the scenario, choosing either from the brainstormed list that the students came up with, or from the suggestions below:

   • faced with a big exam
   • dealing with separation of parents
   • dealing with death of someone close

8) When the students have grouped, have them compare and comment on their choices. Ask them to put their other coping card on top and regroup if they think this card belongs to a different category.

9) Play a few rounds of the game to emphasize the point that different situations may call for different coping strategies. Remind students that there are no right or wrong answers, and that sometimes the most important coping strategy can involve getting help or support for yourself or someone else.

Box Breathing

One useful technique to learn to help with dealing with stress is Box Breathing. It takes about 15 minutes to learn and once mastered can be applied unobtrusively and quietly – ideal for a classroom situation. This technique is described below. Just before beginning the How Do You Cope exercise would be a good time to teach the students Box Breathing.

Box Breathing can help your heart rate return to normal, which helps you to relax. Here's how you do it: If possible, sit and close your eyes. If not, just focus on your breathing.

Step 1: Inhale your breath (preferably through your nose) for 4 seconds.
Step 2: Hold your breath for 4 seconds. You're not trying to deprive yourself of air; you're just giving the air a few seconds to fill your lungs.
Step 3: Exhale slowly through your mouth for 4 seconds.
Step 4: Pause for 4 seconds (without speaking) before breathing again.

Repeat this process as many times as you can. Even 30 seconds of deep breathing will help you feel more relaxed and in control.

Coping Cards

Withdraw – not mix with other people	Think positive about how it will turn out
Play computer games	Worry
Visit a favourite person	See a counselor
Eat more	Eat junk food
Quit (the job, the team…)	Sleep more
Avoid or put off something you have to do	Go for a run
Prioritize (put the most important things first)	Party/socialize
Fantasize - daydream an escape	Run away
Plan – figure out how to do it	Get sick
Start a fight	Blame someone else

Coping Cards

Blame yourself	Smoke cigarettes
Ask for help	Go out
Talk it over	Complain
Eat less	Change direction
Have a shower	Go to bed early
Drink alcohol	Exercise
Work harder	Stay out late
Meditate	Listen to music
Pretend it's okay	Call friends
Watch television	Write about it

MODULE 6

Coping Cards

Cook something	Sleep less
Walk the dog	Go shopping
Pray	Draw or paint
Take a day off	Tidy up
Take risks	Make something
Problem-solve	Find new friends
Cry	Joke or laugh
Set goals	Go for a swim
Play sports	

MODULE 6

Activity 4: (15 mins.)

Taking Charge of My Health

Purpose:

- To reinforce that mental health and physical health are obtained and maintained with numerous similar strategies.

- To provide a diary experience of daily activities needed to obtain and maintain good mental health.

How-to:

1) Introduce the students to the resource Taking Charge of My Health (provide each student with a copy of the resource with enough pages for a week of diary keeping.

2) Instruct each student to every day choose one item from each of the diary sections as their "next day challenge" and to try and complete each of those challenges the next day.

3) Ask the students to do this daily for a week. Also, do it yourself to model how.

4) Review the exercise in a week from now. Lead a classroom discussion: how many challenges did each student manage to keep daily (on average), how did they find the exercise (tiring, difficult, enjoyable, etc.), and what did they learn from doing this exercise?

MODULE 6

Activity 5: (15 mins.)

How Do I Teen My Parent? and How Do I Parent My Teen?

Purpose:

- To provide a vehicle for teens to be able to better understand their parents and their relationship with their parents.

- To encourage the students to discuss issues pertaining to being a teenager and mental health with their parents.

How-to:

1) Download or direct the students to the resource "How do I Teen My Parent" – **http://teenmentalhealth.org/toolbox/teen-parentparent-teen/**.

2) Assign reading the resource for homework – with answers to the following questions to be written down and returned to class.

3) Suggest that they provide their parents with the link to the companion resource "How Do I Parent My Teen".

Homework Questions:

1) What was the most important thing that you learned about being a teenager that you did not already know?

2) What communication tips will you use next time that you have something important to talk to your parent about?

3) Did your parent read the "How do I Parent My Teen" booklet? If so, what did they think of it?

GLOSSARY

Acute: means that something (usually a disorder or a symptom) has come on quickly with a high degree of impact on a person.

Addiction: is continuing to use a substance (for example: alcohol or cocaine) for nonmedical purposes despite wanting or trying to stop using it. Addictions have a negative impact on many areas of a person's functioning in life. For example, if a person's substance use gets in the way of positive relationships with friends or family; success at school or work, it is interfering with their life. An addiction is characterized by: abuse of a chemical; behaviour of drug seeking and daily focus on the drug; craving for the substance. People who are addicted will often experience withdrawal when they stop using a substance. But, withdrawal does not equal addiction. Withdrawal is a common physical response to quickly stopping a chemical that affects the brain.

Agoraphobia: a fear and avoidance of situations where you might feel unsafe or unable to escape if you have a panic attack.

Anhedonia: is a word used to describe a lack of pleasure. Sometimes, people suffering with depression will experience anhedonia. For example, the person doesn't feel good when they are doing the things that normally make them feel good, such as playing a favorite game, swimming, watching movies, etc. Anhedonia due to depression will get better once the depression has been successfully treated.

Anorexia Nervosa (commonly referred to as Anorexia): is a type of eating disorder. The main features that a person with Anorexia will experience are: refusing to maintain a minimally reasonable body weight, intense fear of gaining weight, and an unrealistic perception of their body image (for example: they think or feel that they are much larger or heavier than they actually are.) The word "anorexia" means loss of appetite but many youth with anorexia actually struggle to suppress their appetite. Anorexia Nervosa can be effectively treated with various psychological and family focused therapies.

Antidepressant medicine: a medicine that is usually used to treat the symptoms of depression or anxiety disorders. The antidepressant called "fluoxetine" is considered to be the most useful for helping in adolescent depression. It usually takes 6 to 8 weeks for an antidepressant medicine to work in treating depression.

Anti-social personality disorder: is a type of personality disorder. People with anti-social personality disorder have a long pattern of violating the rights of others. It begins in childhood or early adolescence and continues into adulthood. Other common terms for anti-social personality disorder are sociopath or psychopath. People with this personality disorder will often harm others without feeling remorse or guilt.

140

GLOSSARY

Anxiety: is a type of body signal, or group of sensations that are generally unpleasant. A person with anxiety experiences a variety of physical sensations that are linked with thoughts that make them feel apprehensive or fearful. A person with anxiety will often also think that bad things may happen even when they are not likely to happen. For example, you may be thinking about your puppy falling and getting hurt when it is on the bed and this makes you feel anxious. Anxiety is normal and everyone experiences it. It is a signal that we need to adapt to life's challenges by learning how to cope. When you have so much anxiety that it interferes with your normal routine or many parts of your life such as, school, work, recreation, friends or family — that is when it becomes a problem and maybe even a disorder. Typical sensations of anxiety include: worry, ruminations, "butterflies", twitchiness, restlessness, muscle tension, headaches, dry mouth, feeling as if air is not coming into your lungs, etc.

Anxiety Disorders: are a group of common mental disorders. People with an Anxiety Disorder will experience things like mental and physical tension about their surroundings, apprehension (negative expectations) about the future, and will have unrealistic fears (see anxiety). It is the amount and intensity of the anxiety sensations and how they interfere with life that makes them Disorders. Some common types of Anxiety Disorders are: Social Anxiety Disorder, Panic Disorders, Separation Anxiety Disorder, Generalized Anxiety Disorder, etc. Anxiety Disorders can be effectively treated with psychological therapies or medications.

Asperger's: is often considered to be a developmental disorder that can usually be diagnosed prior to adolescence. People with Asperger's experience repetitive and restrictive behaviours and interests that may lead to impaired functioning at work and socially. Asperger's is considered one of the several disorders on the Autism Spectrum and is unique because there is no significant delay in language development. Many people with Asperger's live full and productive lives without any (or minimal) treatment. Recent research is challenging the idea that Asperger's is a disorder but much more study of this is needed.

Attention Deficit Disorder (ADD): is a term used in the past to diagnose what is now called ADHD (see attention deficit hyper-activity disorder).

Attention Deficit Hyper-Activity Disorder (ADHD): is a mental disorder that is usually lifelong and associated with a delay in how the brain matures and how it processes information. People with ADHD usually have varying degrees of difficulty paying attention, being impulsive, and being over active which causes problems at home, in school, and in social situations. There are three kinds of ADHD: Inattentive Type, Hyperactive-impulsive Type and Combined Type. People with Inattentive Type mostly have problems paying close attention to things or being able to pay attention for long periods of time, so it is harder for them to focus on schoolwork or things that take a lot of concentration for more than a short period of time People with Hyperactive-Impulsive means being on the go and are often not very good about thinking things through before they act.

GLOSSARY

Attention Deficit Hyper-Activity Disorder (ADHD) (Cont.): People with Combined Type have problems with inattention and hyperactivity/impulsivity. ADHD can be treated effectively with medication and behavioural techniques. About 1/3 of young people with ADHD may have a learning disability, so anyone who is diagnosed with ADHD should have special learning tests done.

Antipsychotics: are medicines that are often used to help treat psychosis. Sometimes they can also be used to treat mood swings (such as severe depression or mania) or extreme behaviours (such as aggressive outbursts). This can be confusing if a person is being treated with an antipsychotic medicine and does not have a psychosis. If you are being treated with an antipsychotic medicine make sure you understand why it is being used and its risks and benefits. Check out the "Evidence Based Medicine for Teens" on: www.teenmentalhealth.org.

Affect: Is the emotional experience that someone feels inside of themselves that can be recognized by others. For example: if you are looking/acting sad you can be recognized by someone else as you are feeling sad.

Atypical antipsychotics: are newer types of medicines that help treat psychosis. Sometimes they can be used to treat mood swings (such as severe depression or mania) or extreme behaviours (such as aggressive outbursts). See Antipsychotics above.

Autism Spectrum Disorder (ASD): is a life-long mental disorder in which the person suffers with significant abnormal development of social interaction, verbal and non-verbal communication. A person with Autism has trouble understanding the feelings of others (empathy) and usually does not understand many social norms (rules that tell us what is socially acceptable). Language difficulties range from the inability to speak to automatic sounding repetitive phrases to normal language that sounds formal and emotionless. People with Autism Disorder may also display repetitive behaviours (for example: continuous flapping of hands) and strong need to follow a precise daily schedule and routine. Autism symptoms can vary from extremely severe to mild. Numerous treatments are available to help improve many of the symptoms of Autism, but as of yet there is no single best treatment for Autism. The causes of Autism are complex and not well understood but the popular perception that vaccinations cause Autism is not correct.

Avolition: means having little or no motivation or drive to do things. For example, not getting dressed or not wanting to go out with family or friends. This is not the same thing as "lazy".

Axon: is the long, fibre like part of a nerve cell (neuron) in the brain or spinal cord by which information is carried to other nerve cells.

GLOSSARY

Benzodiazepines: are medications that are used to treat a number of different mental disorders – most commonly anxiety. They can also be used to treat severe restlessness and agitation. When properly used they can be very helpful.

Bipolar Disorder (manic depression): is a mood disorder. People with Bipolar Disorder have experienced at least one full depressive episode and at least one manic episode. Most people with Bipolar Disorder have their first episode before age 25 and it is usually a depression. Bipolar Disorder can be effectively treated with medications and various psychological therapies.

Bipolar Disorder type 2 (hypo-manic depression): is a mood disorder. People with Bipolar Disorder type 2 experience at least one full depressive episode and at least one hypo-manic episode. Hypo-manic episodes are similar to manic episodes but are not as severe. These episodes may last days to months. Bipolar Disorder type 2 can be effectively treated with medications and psychological therapies.

Borderline personality disorder (BPD): is a personality disorder. People with borderline personality disorder have difficulty in regulating their emotions and can experience intense bouts of anger, depression, and anxiety that may last from hours to days or longer. These bouts occur over and over again, often in response to minor life stressors or just on their own. People with BPD have unstable moods, stormy relationships, poor self-image, and self-harming behaviours which can lead to impulsive aggression, self-injury, risk taking and substance abuse.

Brain: is the center of: adaptation, exploration, procreation and civilization. It is the master control of you and your body. You are what your brain is. Your mind is what your brain does. The brain is made up many different parts that are all connected with each other. Here is a very brief overview of some of the parts and some of what they do.

> **Amygdala:** is responsible for emotional memories, responses to fear, emotions and arousal, as well as being involved in the release of hormones that prepare the body for action.

> **Brain stem:** relays messages from the body to the rest of the brain (cerebrum & cerebellum) and vice versa. It also helps control many of the body's vital functions, such as, breathing, digestion, heart rate, sleep and arousal.

> **Cerebellum:** is important for coordinating movement, controlling balance and muscle tone.

GLOSSARY

Brain (Cont.):

Cerebrum: is the largest part of the brain responsible for "higher functions" such as concentration, reason and abstract thinking. It consists of two connected hemispheres (halves) that are divided into the following four lobes:

Frontal lobe: is important in controlling movement, planning behaviour (actions), reasoning, emotions, and problem solving.

Gray matter: is the part of the brain that is dark in color. It is mostly made up of nerve cells (neurons).

Hippocampus: is involved in turning emotional information into memory, learning, and regulating (controlling) emotional responses.

Hypothalamus: communicates with the limbic system to influence behaviour and emotions, controlling body functions such as temperature, sleep, appetite, sexual drive, stress reactions. Also helps control hormone release from the pituitary gland of the brain-endocrine system.

Limbic system: is made up of a group of brain parts that help control emotions, memory, motivation, appetite, and arousal.

Locus Coeruleus: is a small area in the brain stem containing nerve cells that activate the norephrinephrine system that signals anxiety and fear.

Myelin: is a kind of insulation that covers axons and helps nerve signals move more quickly. Myelin is also often called "white matter" because it looks white.

Occipital lobe: is responsible for vision.

Parietal lobe: is responsible for recognition (i.e. knowing what things are), body movement in space, as well as taste and some touch.

Temporal lobe: is important in the processing (i.e. knowing what things mean) and recognition (i.e. knowing what things are) of sounds, as well as, the recognition and memory of objects and faces.

GLOSSARY

Brain (Cont.):

Thalamus: receives information from all parts of the nervous system and relays it to the appropriate parts of the brain that deal with sensation and motor (movement) signals. It also helps to regulate sleep and wakefulness.

To learn more about the brain, check out the brain information sections on this website: www.teenmentalhealth.org.

Bulimia Nervosa: is an eating disorder often just called Bulimia characterized by excessive uncontrollable eating (binges of large amounts of food) over a short period of time, which is then followed by actions that try to get rid of the calories consumed (e.g. vomiting, laxative abuse, excessive exercise). This behaviour is repetitive and often followed by feelings of depression, self-disgust, and guilt. Bulimia can be effectively treated with psychological therapy or medications.

Calorie (also known as kilocalorie): a unit of measurement to calculate heat expenditure or energy. It is often used to determine how much energy is in food or how much energy is used in physical activity. For example an apple may contain 80kcal of energy or a person may use 50kcal walking down stairs.

Cerebellum: look under **Brain**.

Cerebrum: look under **Brain**.

Chronic: means something that is there most of the time for a long time. Often used to describe a disorder that lasts for years or more.

Circadian Rhythm: is the body's biological clock with a cycle of about 24 hours. It helps control our sleep and wake cycle as well as temperature and hormone variations.

Clinic: is a setting where various health professionals work directly with patients.

Clinical: an activity that takes place between a health provider and a patient (for example: diagnosis, treatments, etc.)

Cognition: the mental processes associated with thinking, learning, planning, memory etc.

GLOSSARY

Cognitive Symptoms: are disruptions in normal thoughts. Some medical disorders can interfere with cognition. For example: negative thoughts in depression ("I am a useless person") or delusions (see below) in psychosis ("The FBI is plotting against me") or difficulties in planning or problem solving, etc.

Cognitive Behavioural Therapy: is a form of psychotherapy (talk therapy), designed to help treat various mental disorders. It focuses on changing the persons' thoughts and behaviours to help reverse the person's symptoms and help increase the person's functioning.

Community treatment: this means providing various kinds of treatments and services in the community instead of in the hospital. For example: in the doctor's office, in a health clinic or health center, in a school, etc.

Completed suicide: is the death of a person following a purposeful self-inflicted act with the intent to die. However, a more clear way of saying this is "die by suicide". It is important not to confuse self-harm with suicide attempts.

Computed Axial Tomography (CAT) Scan: is a special kind of X-ray that creates a picture of the structures of the brain – what the brain looks like.

Community Treatment Order: is a legal document that allows or stipulates that a person with a mental disorder will receive treatment while they live in the community.

Comorbidity (also known as dual diagnosis): describes the presence of two disorders that may be associated in a person. For example, someone who has been diagnosed with a Substance Abuse Disorder of Alcohol and Depression.

Compulsions: are repetitive behaviours used to suppress (push out of thought) obsessive thoughts or to follow strong urges. Some types of compulsions include: counting, checking, tapping, etc. While mild and occasional compulsions are common, severe and persistent compulsions can be part of Obsessive Compulsive Disorder.

Concussion: A concussion is a brain injury that is caused by a blow to the head or body that leads to problems with brain function due to brain damage. It can occur without a loss of consciousness and can be caused by what seems to be a mild blow or bump. A concussion can occur in any sport or recreational activity, as a result of a fall or a collision or other mishap. A concussion can lead to many difficulties in thinking, emotions or behaviour and sometimes can lead to a mental disorder such as Major Depressive Disorder or Dysthymia. A concussion requires proper medical treatment. You can find out more about concussions in young people here: www.teenmentalhealth.org.

GLOSSARY

Conduct Disorder (CD): is a disruptive behaviour disorder. The individual with CD shows a persistent pattern of aggressive behaviours lasting over 6 months that are unacceptable to society. Examples include stealing, fighting, starting fires, etc.). Young people with CD often get into difficulty with the law.

Consent: means to give approval or permission to someone to do something. For example a patient must give consent to receive treatment or to be a participant in a research study.

Delusion: is a disturbance of cognition where a person has fixed false beliefs that something has occurred or will occur that is not real. A common delusion is the belief that someone is trying to harm them, even though nobody is. Delusions are often associated with psychosis.

Dendrite: are the specialized fibres that extend from a neuron's cell body and receive messages from other neurons (nerve cells).

Depressant: any substance (medication or drug) that slows down a person's thinking and/or physical functioning. Examples include some pain killers and alcohol.

Depression: is a term used to describe a state of low mood or a mental disorder. This can be confusing because people may often feel depressed but will not have the mental disorder called Depression. People with a Depression could be experiencing either Major Depressive Disorder or Dysthymic Disorder. The most common type of Depression as a mental disorder is a Major Depressive Disorder (MDD). A person with MDD feels very low /sad/depressed or irritable and also experiences: lack of interest, less pleasure, hopelessness, fatigue, sleep problems, loss of appetite, suicidal thoughts. MDD has a negative impact on a person's life, home, family, school/work, friends, etc. Depression can also be part of a Bipolar Disorder (see above). MDD can be effectively treated with psychological therapies or medications.

Depressive Episode: describes a period of depression in MDD or Bipolar Disorder. It includes at least 5 or more of these symptoms being present most of the time, mostly every day for 2 or more weeks: depressed mood, a clear decrease in interest or pleasure in most or all (once enjoyable) activities, a significant weight gain or loss without dieting or loss of appetite, unable to get enough sleep or too much sleep (Insomnia or Hypersomnia), slow movements or purposeless movements from mental tension such as, nervousness or restlessness, which is observable by others (also known as psychomotor agitation or retardation), feeling tired or having less than a normal amount of energy, feeling worthless or a lot of inappropriate guilt, diminished ability to think or concentrate, or indecisiveness (have difficulties making decisions), recurrent (happening again and again) thoughts of death, suicidal ideation (thoughts and/or ideas about death or dying), suicide plan, or suicide attempt.

GLOSSARY

Development: is physical and psychological (emotional and cognitive) growth throughout life.

Diagnosis: is a description that identifies a medical or mental disorder or illness. In North America a diagnosis is determined by the Diagnostic and Statistical Manual of Mental Disorders (DSM) and by the International Classification of Diseases (ICD). A diagnosis is a medical act provided by doctors, psychologists and others trained in diagnosis. A diagnosis is not a label.

Disorder: an abnormality in mental or physical health; disorder is often used as another name for illness.

Distress: is mental or physical suffering. Distress is a part of normal life. Distress is not a mental disorder.

Double Depression: is a mental disorder which is characterized by the presence of both Major Depressive Disorder and a less severe depression known as Dysthymic Disorder in one individual.

DSM IV –TR: is a diagnostic manual published by the American Psychiatry Association that names and describes mental disorders. It divides mental disorders into categories called diagnoses based on lists of criteria (signs and symptoms). Its name is the Diagnostic and Statistical Manual (DSM) the IV-TR refers to the version of the manual as it is updated over time.

Dysthymic Disorder: is a mood disorder. People with Dysthymic Disorder experience persistent low mood for two or more years (or one year for children) but experience fewer depressive symptoms than in Major Depressive Disorder. This low grade depression can result in many difficulties at home, school, work, with family and friends. Dysthymia can be effectively treated with psychology therapies or medication.

Eating Disorders: are a group of mental disorders related to eating. People with (an) eating disorder(s) excessively control their eating, exercise and weight. These disorders include Bulimia, Anorexia Nervosa, Binge Eating Disorder, and Eating Disorder Not Otherwise Specified. Eating disorders can be effectively treated using various psychological and medical treatments.

Electro Convulsive Therapy (ECT): is a form of treatment for mental disorders in which improvements in the disorder are produced by the passage of an electric current through the brain. ETC is given with anesthetic and is most often used to treat severe mood disorders. Its name has the word convulsion in it which means "uncontrollable shaking". This used to occur in the past but does not happen now because the electric current is given while the person is under anesthetic.

GLOSSARY

Electro-Encephalography (EEG): this is a technique that measures the electrical activity occurring in the brain by putting electrodes on top of a person's scalp. It is often used to assess sleep disorders or to diagnose epilepsy.

Euphoria: this word means a much exaggerated sense of happiness or joy. In a mental disorder this can be found in Bipolar Disorder.

Evidence Based Medicine (EDM): is the standard of medical care that happens when the health provider uses the best available scientific information to provide the kind of care the patient needs. For how you can be sure that your health care provider (doctor, nurse, social worker psychologist, etc.) is using EBM check out the EBM materials (for young people and for parents) at **www.teenmentalhealth. org.**

Extraversion: this is personality type where someone is very outgoing and sociable. People with this personality feature are often called "extroverts".

Frontal lobe: look under **Brain**.

Functional Impairment: is a state in which a person is not functioning as they usually would or not functioning well in one or more area of life (i.e. family, friends, intimate relationships, work, school, etc.).

Functional Magnetic Resonance Imaging (FMRI): this is a method for studying how the brain is working. Pictures are taken of different changes that are created when blood flows through different parts of the brain. They help us better understand how the brain works when it is healthy and when it is sick (such as with a mental disorder).

Generalized Anxiety Disorder (GAD): is a mental disorder which is characterized by excessive anxiety and worry about numerous possible events (not any single, specific event) that leads to problems with daily functioning. People with GAD worry all the time and experience many physical symptoms because of the worry (headaches, stomach aches, sore muscles, etc.) GAD can be effectively treated with psychological therapies or medications.

Genetic disposition: this describes the probability that a disorder may be due to genetic factors passed on from parents to their children.

Grandiosity: is having a highly exaggerated and unsubstantiated belief in your importance, ideas or abilities. Unrealistic amounts of grandiosity can be found in Mania and Hypomania.

GLOSSARY

Grief: is normal emotional suffering experienced by a person from a loss of a loved one (e.g. it is experienced when a family member dies). It is different from a depressive disorder. Grief is not a mental disorder.

Hallucination: is a disturbance of how your brain perceived the world. A person with a hallucination experiences senses that aren't real (i.e. sound, sight, smell, taste, or touch). For example, a person with psychosis is hallucinating if they hear voices that aren't occurring in reality.

Health: is a state of physical, mental, social, and spiritual wellbeing and not just the absence of disease or infirmity. It includes mental health.

Health Care Professionals: are the trained professionals who help with the care of people who are sick or who help people and communities stay well. Examples include: doctors, nurses, psychiatrists, psychologists, occupational therapists, social workers, etc.

Hippocampus: look under **Brain**.

Holistic: is used to describe an a type of care that focuses on the whole person, which takes into account their physical and mental state as well as their social background rather than just treating the symptoms of an illness alone.

Hormones: are chemicals formed in one part of the body and carried to another body part or organ where they have an impact on how that part functions. They are important in growth, development, mood, and metabolism (food uptake and break down). For example, serotonin is a hormone in the brain that affects mood, growth hormone comes from the pituitary gland to many parts of the body and affects growth, testosterone affects sexual functioning, etc.

Hospitalization: being kept or staying in a hospital as a patient for doctors and other health care professionals to decide on a diagnosis and implement a treatment plan for the patient. Hospitalization for a mental disorder is usually used only if the disorder is severe or the person is in a crisis situation.

Hypomanic Phase (hypomania): is a milder form of a manic phase. It is usually a part of bipolar disorder. Hypomania can be effectively treated with medication and psychological therapies.

Hypothalamus: look under **Brain**.

Illness: has the same meaning as disease. However, having an illness can mean you have one disease or multiple diseases.

GLOSSARY

International Classification of Diseases of the World Health Organization (ICD): is a book that classifies medical conditions (disorders and diseases) and groups of conditions. These conditions are determined by an international expert committee. This system is used worldwide for all medical diagnoses including mental disorders.

Introversion: means to look inward, for a person to mostly focus on their inner selves and less on their social surroundings. People that have this personality characteristic are often called "introverts".

Involuntary Psychiatric Treatment Act (Nova Scotia): is a law that was passed by Nova Scotia in October 2005. The Act makes sure that those unable to make treatment decisions for themselves, due to their severe mental disorder, receive appropriate treatment. This act is used when someone with and due to a mental disorder:
> a. Has been or is threatening/attempting to be a danger to their self or others OR is likely to suffer serious physical harm or serious mental harm or both.
> b. Does not have the ability to make decisions about their own care.
> c. Requires care in a psychiatric facility and cannot be admitted voluntarily.

Every province in Canada has a similar law.

Involuntary status: is a term used to describe someone who has been admitted into a psychiatric facility (usually a hospital) against their will or without their consent, under the authority and protection of the law.

Knowledge Translation: is similar to changing a document from English to French. It is usually used in reference to changing scientific information into a format that can be easily understood for a specific group of people (e.g. children, adolescents, teachers, adults not in a scientific professional setting, etc.) It is also used to describe how best scientific evidence can be used to improve the care of patients by health professionals.

Locus Coeruleus: look under **Brain**.

Manic Phase: is one of the two phases of bipolar disorder (the other is Depression). It is a period of time during which the person with mania experiences very high energy and excessive activity elevated to the point where they may have difficulty controlling themselves or acting in an expected manner. Three or four of the following symptoms must be present for an episode to be considered to be a manic phase: inflated (really high) self-esteem or grandiosity, decreased need for sleep, more talkative than usual or pressure to keep talking, racing thoughts, distractibility, increase in goal-directed activity, excessive involvement in pleasurable activities that have a potential for painful or negative consequences, such as spending sprees or gambling. A manic phase often requires hospitalization for treatment. It can be effectively treated with medications plus other therapies.

GLOSSARY

Medication: is another word for medicine and is in most cases prescribed by a medical doctor. Medications are regulated by government authorities (in Canada that is Health Canada, in the United States that is the Food and Drug Agency). There are many different classes of medications that are used to treat mental disorders (such as: antidepressants, antipsychotics, anti-anxiety). Medications can also be used to treat specific symptoms that are part of a disorder (such as: aggression).

Mental Disorder: is a disturbance of brain function that meets internationally accepted criteria (DSM or ICD) for a diagnosis. Mental disorders occur as a result of complex interaction between a person's genetic makeup and their environment. Many effective treatments (provided by health professionals) for mental disorders are available. Sometimes people use the term "mental health disorder" when they mean mental disorder. This is not necessary.

Mental Health: is a state of emotional, behavioural, and social wellbeing, not just the absence of mental or behavioural disorder. It does not mean lack of distress. A person can have a mental disorder and mental health at the same time. For example: a person may have a Major Depressive Disorder that has been effectively treated and is still taking treatment for the disorder. Now they have mental health as well as a mental disorder.

Mental Health Issue: is a broad term used to describe mental distress, mental suffering or mental disorder. It is so broad that many researchers and health professionals think it is meaningless. We advise not using this term, but instead being clear about what you are talking about.

Mental Health Nurse (clinical nurse with a specialty in psychiatry): is a registered nurse who specializes in the maintenance of mental health and the treatment of mental disorders. This type of nurse usually works directly with people in a clinical setting, such as in a hospital or community clinic. Mental Health nurses have many skills used in the diagnosis and treatment of people with mental disorders.

Mental Health Professional: is a broad category of health care workers who work to help other people improve their mental health or treat mental disorders. Examples are psychiatrists, clinical social workers, psychiatric nurses, psychologists, mental health counselors, child and youth workers, etc. They have all received training in working with people who are living with a mental disorder.

Mental Health Promotion: these are activities that try to improve the mental health of people or try to reduce risk for the development of various mental health or social problems.

GLOSSARY

Mental Illness: refers to a range of brain disorders that affect mood, behaviour, and thought process. Mental illnesses are listed and defined in the DSM and the ICD. The terms mental illness and mental disorder are often used interchangeably.

Mental retardation: is the below average general mental functioning that can be first noticed during childhood and is associated with problems in adjusting to different environments. A diagnosis of mental retardation means that the person has shown to perform lower than average (compared to others their age) in two areas: measured intelligence (IQ) and an overall rating of the individual's level of performance in school, at work, at home and in the community.

Mood: is the ongoing inner emotional feeling experienced by a person.

Mood Disorders: are a group of mental disorders related to problems in how the brain is controlling emotions. A person with a mood disorder experiences an abnormal change in mood. These include: MDD, Bipolar Disorder, and Dysthymia.

Mood stabilizers: medicines used to help normalize mood. They are usually used to treat Bipolar Disorder. Some of these are: lithium, valproate, carbamezapine. Some of these medicines are also commonly used in the treatment of epilepsy.

Myelin: look under **Brain**.

Narcissistic: is a quality or trait of a person who interprets and regards everything in relation to their own self and not to other people. It is associated with an unrealistic and highly inflated self worth.

Negative symptoms: are symptoms of Schizophrenia that follow a lessening of executive functioning (conscious choice, intention, decision making; problem solving) in the brain. The person either has less of something (for example energy) or is unable to do something (for example, unable to get out of bed). These symptoms include: inertia (inability to get one's self going), lack of energy, lack of interaction with their friends and family members, poverty of thought (significantly fewer thoughts), social withdrawal, and blunted affect (less emotionally responsive).

Neurodevelopment: is how the brain grows and changes over time.

Neuron (nerve cell): is a unique type of cell found in the brain and the spinal cord that processes and transmits information within the nervous system.

Neuroscience: is the scientific study of the brain and the nervous system.

GLOSSARY

Neurotransmission: is the process that occurs when a neuron releases special chemicals called neurotransmitters that relay a signal to another neuron across the synapse (a gap between parts of nerve cells).

Neurotransmitters: are chemicals used to communicate messages that are being sent from one brain cell to another in the spaces between those cells. When the production, release, or uptake of any of these chemicals is impaired the brain may show problems in how it is working. Some examples of neurotransmitters are: dopamine, serotonin, noradrenalin, etc.

Obsessions: are repetitive, persistent, unwanted thoughts that the person cannot stop and which cause significant distress and impair the person's ability to function. Mild and occasional obsessive thoughts are normal, but when they become severe and persistent they can be part of Obsessive Compulsive Disorder.

Obsessive-Compulsive Disorder (OCD): is a type of mental disorder. People with obsessive compulsive disorder experience persistent unwanted and recurring thoughts (obsessions) and/or persistent and unwanted repetitive behaviours (compulsions). Repetitive behaviours are carried out with the goal of preventing or getting rid of the obsessions or of releasing a strong feeling of inner tension. These behaviours may provide temporary relief for the person while not performing them can cause extreme anxiety. Examples of obsessions include repetitive thoughts of germs or contamination. Examples of compulsions include repetitive or excessive touching, counting, hand washing, and cleaning. OCD can be effectively treated with medications and psychological therapies.

Occupational Therapist: is a trained health professional that focuses on increasing a person's independent functioning, improving social skills, and preventing disability using self-care, employment, and recreational (fun) activities. For example, helping someone with a mental or physical disability develop job competencies or improve their daily living skills.

P.R.N. (as needed): is a Latin abbreviation used for prescriptions. Pro re nata, translates to: when necessary.

Panic Attack: is a sudden experience of intense fear or psychological and physical discomfort that develops for no apparent reason and that includes physical symptoms such as dizziness, trembling, sweating, difficulty breathing or increased heart rate. Occasional panic attacks are normal. If they become persistent and severe, the person can develop a Panic Disorder.

GLOSSARY

Panic Disorder: is a mental disorder. A person with panic disorder has panic attacks, expects and fears the attacks and avoids going to places where escape may be difficult if a panic attack happens. Sometimes, people with Panic Disorder can develop Agoraphobia. Panic Disorder can be effectively treated with psychological therapies or medications.

Patient advocate: is a person who helps a patient (or a patient's family) with problems and complaints in relation to care or help that they are getting from any agency or institution (hospital, clinic, psychiatric clinic, etc.) Patient advocates can speak on behalf of the patient (or family) and can often be helpful during times of disagreement between the patient (or family) and health care professionals. Many hospitals employ people who act as patient advocates.

Perception: is the mental process of becoming aware of or recognizing information that comes from the five senses: sight, sound, smell, touch or taste. Proprioception (knowing where your body parts are without looking) is also a type of perception.

Personality Disorders: is a general term for a group of behavioural disorders characterized by lifelong behaviour patterns. People with Personality Disorders don't adjust or function well in changing social environments. Signs of these patterns may include poor judgment, emotional control, impulse control, relationship functioning, etc.

Positive symptoms: are symptoms found in psychosis, often in Schizophrenia. They include hallucinations, delusions, loose associations (unclear connections between ideas or disorganized flow of conversation topics), ambivalence (wanting to act one way but act in a way that is opposite to that), or unstable or quickly changing emotions.

Positron Emission Tomography (PET) scans: a technique using radioactive substances for studying how the brain is working by measuring different chemicals involved in the brain's work.

Postsynaptic neuron: is the nerve cell (neuron) that receives messages from other neurons across a synapse.

Posttraumatic Stress Disorder (PTSD): This mental disorder can happen to people who experience a really scary, painful, or horrific event in which they felt scared or helpless and during which they were in danger of death or severe injury. People who develop PTSD will have flashback memories, or nightmares, of the event and will avoid things that remind them of the event. For example, if a person was assaulted in a park they may be too fearful to go to parks and have to find new routes to work. PTSD can be effectively treated with psychological interventions or medications.

GLOSSARY

Presynaptic neuron: is the nerve cell (neuron) that sends messages to other neurons across a synapse.

Prognosis: is an educated guess, based on previous evidence and scientific study, of how the disorder will affect the person over time. Your health provider will estimate the length of time the disorder will be present and how it may affect you. A prognosis can change over time. For example, if a treatment is very helpful then the prognosis may improve.

Protective factor: is anything that decreases a person's chances of getting a disorder or having a negative outcome. Protective factors can be aspects of a person's health, lifestyle or environment, such as a supporting family or community. Their actual effect in any one person is not easy to predict and it is not clear if they all actually have a direct effect or are just examples taken from healthy people compared to people who are not well.

Psychiatrist: is a doctor who specializes in the practice of psychiatry (the treatment of people who have a mental disorder and the prevention of mental disorders). Psychiatrists are medical doctors who have had many years of additional training in psychiatric medicine.

Psychiatry: is the medical specialty focused on understanding, diagnosing and treating mental disorders.

Psychologist: is a Ph. D level specialist in psychology licensed to practice professional psychology (e.g. clinical psychology), or qualified to teach psychology as a discipline
(academic psychology), or whose scientific specialty is a subfield of psychology (research psychology).

Psychomotor: describes the mental process that helps put physical movements into action. For example, a feeling of fatigue may lead to walking very slowly or resting on a couch.

Psychomotor agitation: are movements that happen because of mental tension. It is often described as a way of relieving mental tension. For example, pacing back and forth and peeling or biting skin around fingers.

Psychomotor retardation: are slow thoughts as well as movements that are slowed down.

GLOSSARY

Psychosis: is a mental state in which a person has lost the ability to recognize reality. Symptoms can vary from person to person but may include changes in thinking patterns, delusions, hallucinations, changes in mood, or difficulty completing everyday tasks (like bathing or shopping). Mental disorders such as Schizophrenia can include psychosis as a symptom. Psychosis can be effectively treated with medications and other additional treatments.

Psychotherapy: is a type of treatment for emotional, behavioural, personality, and other psychiatric disorders based mainly on person to person communication. Psychotherapies can be evidence based (supported by many good research studies) or non-evidence based (not supported by many good research studies). It is important for a patient to know what the evidence to support the psychotherapy that they are being treated with is. To find out more about any psychotherapy, check out the Evidence Based Medicine booklet at: www.teenmentalhealth.org.

Receptor: is a special part of a neuron where different chemicals from other neurons (neurotransmitters) or medicines attach, leading to messages going between neurons being sent or blocked.

Recreation Therapist: is a professional that is trained in the specific area of therapy that uses recreational and leisure methods, such as games and activities, to improve a person's physical, mental, emotional, and relationship functioning.

Recreation Therapy: is a type of therapy that uses methods such as games and group activities to improve a person's physical, mental, emotional, and relationship functioning.

Recovery: is when a person with a mental disorder is doing as well as they can be and is feeling mentally healthy – even if they still have a mental disorder.

Relapse: is when a person with a mental disorder who has been in remission or recovery gets sick again.

Remission: is when a person's symptoms decrease and they return to their usual state after having an active phase of a disorder.

Research: is the in-depth study done on a topic to find an answer to a question (e.g. a study on what is the best treatment for Depression). There are many types of research approaches used: (for example observational, analytical, experimental, theoretical, and applied). Not all research is of the same value. One type of research design called the Randomized Controlled Trial (RCT) is the gold standard for helping us find out what treatments work best.

GLOSSARY

Results: are the outcomes of a study that support or do not support what the researchers had thought. They are use to guide practice or support further research.

Risk factor: is anything that increases a person's chances of getting a disorder (can be aspects of a person's health, genetics, lifestyle or environment). Remember, risk factors increase a person's chances of getting a disorder – they do not cause the disorder. And, risk factors can be weak or strong. So having a specific risk factor may or may not be important for the person.

Safety: is the potential of a treatment or therapy to lead to or cause serious negative effects.

Schizoaffective Disorder: is a psychotic disorder that has symptoms of both Schizophrenia and a major mood disorder. People with Schizoaffective disorder can be effectively treated with medications and other additional treatments.

Schizophrenia: is a mental disorder that can usually be diagnosed between the ages of 15 and 25. People who have Schizophrenia experience delusions and hallucinations (psychotic symptoms) and many other problems that can make day to day living difficult. While Schizophrenia runs in families some people can get Schizophrenia without a family history of the disorder. Schizophrenia can be treated with medications and additional interventions that can improve the lives of people with the disorder.

Seasonal Affective Disorder (SAD): is a type of Major Depressive Disorder that usually happens to people only or mostly at certain times of year (for example: winter).

Selective Serotonin Reuptake Inhibitors (SSRIs): are a group of medications used to treat depression. These medications work mainly in the serotonin system of the brain.

Self–harm: is any injury that a person inflicts on themselves without the intent to die. Examples of self- harming behaviours include: burning or cutting following an emotionally upsetting event, burning or cutting as a method of manipulation or threat, burning or cutting as a way of solving a problem.

Separation Anxiety Disorder: is an Anxiety Disorder that can be diagnosed in children which makes it very hard for them to be away from their parent. People with Separation Anxiety Disorder can be helped with psychological treatments.

GLOSSARY

Serotonin: is a neurotransmitter that helps in regulating many different brain functions, including mood, anxiety and thinking.

Single Photon Emission Computed Tomography (SPECT): is a technique that is used to study how the brain is functioning.

Social: is the ability to interact with other people in ways that are commonly accepted and appropriate to the situation/culture.

Social Phobia (also known as Social Anxiety Disorder): is an anxiety disorder regarding the fear of having to be in social situations. A person with Social Anxiety Disorder also avoids the situations that make them feel anxious. Examples include, the fear of public speaking, the fear of going to a party because other people are "judging" them, performing in front of other people. People with Social Anxiety Disorder can be effectively treated with psychotherapy or medication.

Social Worker: is a professional who is educated to deal with social, emotional, and environmental problems that may be associated with a disorder or disability. Services provided by social workers may include case management (connecting patients with programs that meet their needs), counseling, human service management, social welfare policy analysis, and policy and practice development.

Sociopath (or psychopath): is a person with antisocial personality disorder.

Socipathy: are the behaviour patterns and personality traits a sociopath displays such as superficial (fake) charm, having a lack of remorse (doesn't feel badly/guilty about doing something wrong), and others.

Somatic: describes the physical body. For example: sore muscles, fatigue, and headache are all somatic (also known as physical) sensations.

Specific Phobia: is an Anxiety Disorder. A person with a specific phobia experiences fear in the presence of an object or situation, snakes, fear of heights, fear of the dark, etc. Specific phobias often do not need to be treated. If they do, behaviour therapy is usually used.

St. John's Wort: is an herb that some people think can help treat Depression. It is not approved by Health Canada for use in treating mental disorders.

GLOSSARY

Stigma related to mental illness: is attaching negative qualities to mental disorders (for example, thinking people with a mental disorder are dangerous). Stigma is a strong force and is harmful in that it may keep people from speaking about their disorder, getting help, or receiving treatment. It can create a false image of what mental disorders are and may force people to limit their social interactions, work, education, or to not seek help if they have a mental disorder.

Stress: is the body's reaction when forces such as infections or toxins disrupt the body's normal physiological equilibrium (homeostasis). Psychological stress develops in response to when a person perceives a threat, real or imagined, and determines whether they have the skills or resources to cope with the perceived threat. Stress is necessary for learning how to adapt. Too much stress can lead to a variety of health problems.

Stimulants: are a group of medications that improve various aspects of brain function: such as: alertness, concentration, etc. They are often used to treat ADHD.

Substance abuse: is an unhealthy pattern of drug, alcohol or other chemical use that may lead to relationship, education, work, mental and/or physical problems.

Substance dependence: is a pattern of actions, physical, and mental symptoms that develop from abuse of a substance (drug). A person who has a substance dependency may develop tolerance to the substance's effects and may experience withdraw symptoms when they stop using the substance. They crave the substance and engage in behaviour designed to access and use the substance – even if the behaviour or substance is harmful to them. A similar term is "Addiction".

Substitute decision maker: is a person who is given the authority to make care or treatment decisions on behalf of an involuntary patient. See Involuntary Treatment Act.

Suicide: is death that occurs as a result of an action designed to end one's life.

Suicidality: refers to any thoughts or actions associated with the desire or intent to die. We do not recommend using this term as it is so broad that it cannot convey clearly what a person means. For example: a passing thought about death or an attempt to die are both examples of suicidality.

GLOSSARY

Suicide Attempt: a purposeful act with the intent to end one's life that does not cause death.

Suicidal Ideation: refers to thoughts, images or fantasies of harming or killing oneself.

Suicidal intent: is the commitment and expectation of death by suicide. (Future tense: the person intends to take their life. Past tense: the person intended to take their life).

Suicidal Plan: is the mentally created plan to attempt to end one's life

Supported decision making: is the process in which a vulnerable person is provided advice, support, and assistance by their support network so they can make and communicate their own decisions.

Symptom: is an occurrence of any type experienced by a person that differs from their normal in structure, behaviour, sensation, emotion or cognition that indicates illness or disease.

Synapse or synaptic space: is a space between neurons (nerve cells). Neurons release chemicals into this space that regulate how messages in the brain operate.

Syndrome: is a collection of signs (what a person observes about another person) and symptoms (what a person experiences) that describes a disease.

Systematic Desensitization: is a type of psychological treatment which gradually introduces things that a person fears so that they gradually overcome their fears.

Teen mental health: is a teen's state of emotional and spiritual wellbeing and not just the absence of disease. Focusing to improve the mental health and ability of teens' academic, social, physical, and other functioning will, in turn, increase their ability to contribute to society in the short term and in the long term in meaningful ways it is based on the brains ability to adapt.

Therapist: is a person who is professionally trained and/or skilled in the practice of a particular type of therapy.

Therapy: is the treatment of disease or disorder by any method.

Tolerance: is when a person becomes less responsive to a medication or other treatment over time.

GLOSSARY

Trauma: is any painful or damaging injury or event-that harms a person's physical or mental health.

Treatment: medical, psychological, social or surgical management and care of a patient.

Trichotillomania: is a mental disorder. People with Trichotillomania pull out their hair over and over again leaving noticeable hair loss. The person usually experiences tension before pulling the hair or if they try to stop themselves from pulling the hair and feel either pleasure or relief when pulling the hair out. The location of the hair can be anywhere on the body but is commonly from the scalp, eyebrows and eyelashes. Psychological treatments and sometimes medications are usually used to help with this disorder.

Violence: is emotional, sexual and/or physical abuse towards someone usually in an effort to gain power or control of another person or group of people.

Voluntary admission: is being admitted as a patient to a mental health unit for treatment (usually in a hospital) based on a person's agreement to be admitted.

Voluntary patient: is a person who stays in a psychiatric facility (usually a hospital) by their own consent or with the consent of the substitute decision maker.

Withdrawal: is a brain response to a sudden stopping of use of a medication or drug. Symptoms of withdrawal can include: nausea, chills, cramps, diarrhea, hallucinations, etc. Withdrawal often occurs in addiction / substance dependence but most people who experience it are not addicted. Another meaning of withdrawal is the self directed avoidance of social contact. This can be seen in some mental disorders such as: Depression, Schizophrenia, Panic Disorder, etc.

References

DSM IV-TR, Diagnostic and statistical manual of mental disorders, Fourth Edition, Text Revision.

Washington, DC: American Psychiatric Association, 2000.

Pugh, M. B. (Ed.). (2000). Stedman's Medical Dictionary. Baltimore, Maryland: Lippincott

Williams and Wilkins.

COMMUNITY MENTAL HEALTH RESOURCE LIST

Community Mental Health Resources

The following mental health related resources are available in many communities. Find out the contact information for these resources in your community and distribute to students.

Kids Help Phone – 1-800-668-6868

Kids Help Phone is Canada's only 24-hour, national bilingual telephone counseling service for children and youth. Provides counseling directly to children and youth directly between the ages of 4 and 19 years and helps adults aged 20 and over to find the counseling services they need.

Parents, teachers and any other concerned adults are welcome to call for information and referral services at any time.

Local Distress lines _____

Local Mental Health Organizations_____

Canadian Mental Health Association

For information about the CMHA Branch in your area, please see the CMHA National website at **www.cmha.ca**

Schizophrenia Society

For information about your local Schizophrenia Society Chapter, please see their website at **www.schizophrenia.ca**

Local Community Mental Health Clinic _____

Local Community Health Centre_____

Local Hospital_____

WEBSITE RESOURCES FOR TEACHERS

Further Information on Mental Health Problems and Mental Illness:

American Academy of Child and Adolescent Psychiatry
http://www.aacap.org/

The AACAP website contains a wide range of information on childhood and adolescent mental health and illness geared toward different audiences, including educators and parents.

Canadian Centre on Substance Abuse
www.ccsa.ca

The CCSA website contains a wide array of information and resources on substance abuse with the intention of reducing the harm of alcohol and other drugs on society.

Canadian Mental Health Association
www.cmha.ca

CMHA National has a comprehensive range of information available to download from their website, including a complete series of pamphlets with vital information on mental health and mental illness.

Additionally, you will find many resources pertaining to mental health and high school for teachers, parents and students at www.cmha.ca/highschool

The Dana Foundation
www.dana.org

The Dana Foundation is a private philanthropic organization that supports brain research through grants, publications, and educational programs. They are committed to advancing brain research and to educating the public in a responsible manner about the potential of research.

Kelty Mental Health – Anxiety in the Classroom: Resource for Teachers
www.keltymentalhealth.ca/sites/default/files/Summer%20Institute%202011%20-%20Resource%20List%20ANXIETY.pdf

A list of resources for teachers on how to manage and reduce anxiety in the classroom setting.

MindMatters
www.mindmatters.edu.au

A resource and professional development program to support Australian secondary

WEBSITE RESOURCES FOR TEACHERS

schools in promoting and protecting the social and emotional wellbeing of members of school communities.

National Institute for Drug Abuse (NIDA)
www.drugabuse.gov

The NIDA website contains up-to date and reliable information about a wide range of issues relating to drug abuse.

National Institute for Mental Health (NIMH)
www.nimh.nih.gov/

The NIMH website contains up-to date and reliable information about a wide range of issues relating to mental health and illness across the lifespan.

Reaching Out
www.schizophrenia.ca/reaching.php

A complete, easy to teach, bilingual educational program specially created for Canadian youth. The program includes classroom activities and a video which provide information on Psychosis and Schizophrenia.

When Something's Wrong: Strategy's for Teachers
www.healthymindscanada.ca/when-somethings-wrong-handbook

A quick reference source of useful classroom strategies to help elementary and secondary school teachers and administrators understand and assist students with mood, behaviour or thinking disorders.

Available from Healthy Minds Canada

Information Geared to Young People:

Mind Check
www.mindcheck.ca

Mindcheck.ca is a place where youth can get information, resources, take quizzes and get informed on tools to help manage stress, crisis and mental health problems.

Mind your Mind
www.mindyourmind.ca/

Mindyourmind.ca is a place where youth can get information, resources and the tools to help manage stress, crisis and mental health problems.

WEBSITE RESOURCES FOR TEACHERS

Psychosis Sucks
www.earlypsychosis.ca

This site contains valuable information for youth in the importance of early intervention in psychosis. It includes information on warning signs and how to get help, along with personal stories and accounts of recovery.

General Mental Health Websites:

Kelty Mental Health Resource Centre
http://www.keltymentalhealth.ca/

Teen Mental Health (Sun Life Financial Chair in Adolescent Mental Health IWK/Dalhousie University)
http://www.teenmentalhealth.org/

PUBLICATIONS ABOUT THE GUIDE

1. McLuckie, A., Kutcher, S., Wei, Y., & Weaver, C. (2015). Sustained improvements of students' mental health literacy with use of a mental health curriculum in Canadian schools. BMC Psychiatry, 14: 379.

2. Wei, Y., Kutcher, S., Heather, H., & Mackay, A. (2014). Successfully embedding mental health literacy into Canadian classroom curriculum by building on existing educator competencies and school structures: the Mental Health and High School Curriculum Guide for secondary schools in Nova Scotia. Literacy Information and Computer Education Journal, 5 (3): 1158-1163

3. Kutcher, S., & Wei, Y. (2014). School mental health literacy: a national curriculum guide shows promising results. Education Canada, 54 (2), 22-25

4. Kutcher, S., Wei, Y., McLuckie, A., & Bullock, L. (2013). Educator mental health literacy: a program evaluation of the teacher training education on the Mental Health & High School Curriculum Guide. Advances in School Mental Health Promotion, 10, 1-11.

5. Kutcher, S., Doucet, L., & Wei, Y. (2012). Mental Health and High School Curriculum Guide – a mental health literacy program for Canadian educators and youth. The Register of Ontario Principals' Council, Winter.

Printed in Great Britain
by Amazon